TRIAL EVIDENCE --

MAKING AND MEETING OBJECTIONS

MSU/DETROIT COLLEGE OF LAW

NATIONAL INSTITUTE FOR TRIAL ADVOCACY

EDUCATIONAL SERVICES COMMITTEE

Kenneth S. Broun, Chair
Henry Brandis Professor of Law
University of North Carolina School of Law
Chapel Hill, North Carolina

James E. Ferguson, II
Ferguson, Stein, Watt, Wallas, Adkins &
Gresham, P.A.
Charlotte, North Carolina

Joseph C. Jaudon
Long & Jaudon, P.C.
Denver, Colorado

Louise A. LaMothe
Irell & Manella
Los Angeles, California

Richard M. Markus
Porter, Wright, Morris & Arthur
Cleveland, Ohio

Rudolph F. Pierce
Goulston & Storrs
Boston, Massachusetts

TRIAL EVIDENCE--

MAKING AND MEETING OBJECTIONS

by

Anthony J. Bocchino
Professor of Law
Temple University

David A. Sonenshein
Professor of Law
Temple University

JoAnne Epps
Associate Professor of Law
Temple University

SECOND EDITION
1990

Copies of this case file are available from the National Institute for Trial Advocacy. Please direct inquiries to:

>John R. Kouris, Chief Operating Officer
>National Institute for Trial Advocacy
>Notre Dame Law School
>Notre Dame, Indiana 46556
>(800) 225-6482
>FAX (219) 282-1263

Bocchino, Sonenshein, and Epps, <u>Trial Evidence: Making and Meeting Objections</u>, 2nd ed., (NITA, 1990).

ISBN 1-55681-2337

TO LYNN, JENNY AND JAY

A.J.B.
D.A.S.
J.A.E.

ACKNOWLEDGMENTS

The authors thank Dean Bob Reinstein of the Temple University School of Law for his support of this project. Also thanks to Eartha Nesmith for her patience throughout the many revisions, and David Bogan of the Law School Secretarial Support Center, who assisted in several rewrites.

Finally, and most importantly, we thank our Evidence students who inspired these materials and served as editors and critiquers of our work.

Anthony J. Bocchino
David A. Sonenshein
JoAnne Epps

TRIAL EVIDENCE--

MAKING AND MEETING OBJECTIONS

Second Edition

<u>TABLE OF CONTENTS</u>

INTRODUCTION

This book contains 64 vignettes of trial testimony designed to raise evidentiary issues in the context in which they occur. Each raises at least one evidentiary issue, although most vignettes have broader coverage.

These materials can be viewed in both an evidence or trial advocacy class, or as the basis for continuing legal education on evidence. In the law school setting, they will serve as supplementary materials, to be used in conjunction with a book, problem book, or casebook. The vignettes are examples of how specific evidentiary issues arise at trial, and provide context for a better understanding of the rules of evidence as they are applied.

Each vignette begins with a short description of a lawsuit during which the vignette testimony occurs. A transcript of the text of a witness testimony in that lawsuit, in the question and answer format, follows. Transcripts beginning with a "Q2:" denote statements, objections, or arguments made by opposing counsel. Transcripts beginning with an "A:" denote answers by the witness.

Periodic pauses are noted in each vignette. At each pause, consideration should be given as to whether an objection can be made to the questions, answers, or rulings that precede the pause, the grounds for that objection, the appropriate response to that objection, and the proper ruling by a judge. If an objection would be properly sustained, consideration should then be given as to whether that objection could be cured by the laying of an evidentiary foundation.

During class students will normally be assigned to play the roles of questioning attorney and witness. As the transcript is read, either a particular student or the rest of the class is assigned to make objections and arguments on those objections as necessary. If the objection is curable, questioning counsel is called upon to perform that function. The role of the judge is usually taken by the course instructor, but it can also be assigned.

As the vignettes are played out in class, the student should stay in role as trial counsel and make objections and arguments as they would in court. A full discussion raised by each vignette can occur at the end of the vignette or at each pause, at the option of the instructor. Space is provided on the materials for note-taking concerning objections, responses, and rulings.

Anthony J. Bocchino

Vignette 1

The plaintiff, John Bernstein, has sued the defendant, Mary Wilson, for injuries he received when he was hit by her car as he crossed Main Street near the intersection of 7th Avenue in Nita City. Bernstein claims that Wilson was negligent in that she was driving in excess of the 20 mph speed limit that exists in all business districts in Nita City and further that she was driving too fast for conditions. Wilson claims that Bernstein was responsible for his own injuries in that he crossed Main Street without using the crosswalk. The first witness for the plaintiff is Officer Nancy Wright, who investigated the incident. We pick up in the midst of Wright's testimony.

Q: Directing your attention to April 3rd of YR-3, were you on duty that day?

A: Yes, I was working as a patrol officer on the 8:00 a.m. to 4:00 p.m. shift.

Q: What happened at approximately 3:00 p.m.?

A: I got a call to investigate a car-pedestrian accident near the intersection of 7th and Main in Nita City.

Q: Have you ever been to that intersection before?

A: Yes, many times. It's in my patrol area.

Q: What is located at that intersection?

A: It is a mixed commercial and residential area.

Q: Your Honor, I ask that you take judicial notice of the fact that the intersection of 7th Avenue and Main Street is a business district.

A: I object, your Honor. May we offer evidence on this point?

Judge: Counselor, I've lived in Nita City all of my life and I can tell you from personal experience that the intersection of 7th Avenue and Main Street is a business district.

(Pause - 1)

Q: What did you find at the intersection, Officer
     Wright?

A: The plaintiff, Mr. Bernstein, was lying on the
     pavement. He appeared to be unconscious. The
     defendant was standing near him.

Q: What were the weather conditions at that time?

A: I really don't remember.

Q: Your Honor, I ask that you take judicial notice of
     the fact that on April 3, YR-3, it rained all
     afternoon in Nita City.

     (Pause - 2)

Q: Do you know the speed limit on Main Street at the
     intersection of 7th Avenue?

A: I know what it is now but I can't be sure that it
     was the same three years ago.

Judge: I drive by that intersection every day and the speed
     limit is 20 mph. To save time, I'll take judicial
     notice of that fact.

     (Pause - 3)

<u>**Vignette 2**</u>

On May 1st at approximately 11:30 a.m. the plaintiff, John Parsons, and the defendant, Rachel Dornan, were involved in a car accident at the intersection of 68th Street and Sherwood Avenue. The plaintiff claims that the defendant, while driving west on Sherwood Avenue in her Dodge van, ran a red light and struck the plaintiff's Toyota, which was traveling north on 68th Street. The defendant claims that she entered the intersection on a yellow light and in fact the plaintiff ran the red light.

The first witness for the plaintiff is the plaintiff, John Parsons.

Q: What is your name?

A: John Parsons.

Q: Where do you live?

A: 7000 Greenhill Road here in town.

Q: And you've lived there for the past ten years?

    (Pause - 1)

A: That's right.

Q: What do you do for a living?

A: I work for the city as a maintenance worker. I've been doing that for eight years since I graduated from high school.

Q: Directing your attention to May 1st of last year at about 11:30 a.m., where were you?

A: In my car driving north on 68th Street in the city.

Q: How fast were you driving?

A: I can't put a number on it, but not very fast.

    (Pause - 2)

Q: Were you driving within the posted speed limit of 35 miles per hour?

(Pause - 3)

A: Sure, no question about it.

Q: O.K., what happened when you got to the intersection of 68th Street and Sherwood?

(Pause - 4)

A: Well, as I approached the intersection the light was red for the northbound traffic, but about 100 feet before I reached Sherwood the light changed to green for the 68th Street traffic so I just kept on going.

Q: So you had the green light and weren't speeding?

(Pause - 5)

A: Yes, definitely.

Q: What happened next?

A: Just as I entered the intersection my car was hit by that careless Dornan in the Dodge van coming from the east to west.

(Pause - 6)

Q: What part of your car did the defendant hit when she ran the red light?

A: The right front quarter panel.

Q: Did you get the car repaired?

A: Yes, of course.

Q: How much did it cost to repair the car?

A: I don't remember specifically.

Q: Would it refresh your recollection if I told you it was $1420.50?

(Pause - 7)

A: No, but it's on the bill from the repair shop.

Q: Showing you that bill do you now remember the specific amount?

(Pause - 8)

A: (Reading from bill) Yes, it says here $1,420.50.

(Pause - 9)

Q: Was all that damage caused by the defendant speeding through the red light?

(Pause - 10)

A: Yes.

Q: Is there any question in your mind that you had a green light and the defendant ran a red light?

(Pause - 11)

A: None whatsoever.

Cross-Examination of the Plaintiff, Parsons

Q: You aren't sure about your exact speed at the time of the accident, are you?

A: Well, I know that I was going under the speed limit.

(Pause - 12)

Q: You were on your way to a doctor's appointment at the time of the accident?

A: That's right.

Q: The appointment was for 11:30, wasn't it?

A: Yes, but he's always late.

    (Pause - 13)

Q: You were going to see the doctor for migraine headaches, right?

A: Yes.

Q: A dog crossed your path right before the accident, correct?

A: Yes.

Q: You swerved to avoid the dog, right?

A: Yes, but that didn't have anything to do with the accident.

    (Pause - 14)

Q: But in addition to being late for a doctor's appointment and suffering a migraine headache, you did swerve to avoid the dog, didn't you?

    (Pause - 15)

A: That's not right.

Q: The jury will decide the facts sir, nothing further.

    (Pause - 16)

Vignette 3

The plaintiff, Maria Rodriguez, has sued the defendant, Business Machines Incorporated (BMI), for discrimination on the basis of gender and national origin in the making of a promotion decision. She claims that she was passed over for a promotion to Assistant Vice-President for Sales from her position as Sales Manager for the Eastern Region of BMI because of her national origin. The events underlying this cause of action happened in YR-2. The plaintiff is the first witness at trial.

Q: Please state your name and address for the record.

A: Maria Rodriguez, 7000 Sherwood Lane, Nita City, Nita.

Q: What is your occupation?

A: I am the Sales Manager for the Eastern Region of BMI.

Q: You've had that position for six years, haven't you?

(Pause - 1)

A: Yes.

Q: What education do you have that prepared you for that position?

A: I graduated from the Nita City public schools, and received my B.S. in business and M.B.A. from Nita University.

Q: I take it from your last response that you are a lifelong resident of Nita City?

(Pause - 2)

A: Yes, that's right.

Q: When did you start working for BMI?

A: In YR-15, after I received my MBA.

Q: How many promotions have you received at BMI?

(Pause - 3)

A: Four, from Sales Assistant to Assistant Sales
Manager to Division Sales Manager to Assistant
Regional Sales Manager to Regional Sales Manager, my
current position.

Q2: Objection. I move to strike all of the previous
answer after "four" as non-responsive.

(Pause - 4)

Q: Is Assistant Vice-President for Sales the next
position up the chain of responsibility from your
current position?

(Pause - 5)

A: Yes.

Q: Directing your attention to August of YR-2, did you
apply for the position of Assistant Vice-President
of Sales at BMI?

A: Yes.

Q: Did you fill out the necessary papers and forward
them to the powers that be?

(Pause - 6)

A: Yes, I followed the procedure set out in the
position announcement.

Q: What papers did you have to submit to the President
of BMI?

(Pause - 7)

A: A resume and a brief statement of what I felt were
my qualifications for the position.

Q: Was the next step in the process--to go through
interviews?

(Pause - 8)

A: Yes.

Q: What happened during the interviewing process?

(Pause - 9)

A: The first round of interviews was routine. The questions were tough but fair and I was confident that I was doing pretty well. The next and final step was an interview with the President, Mr. Stenton. During that interview he seemed to be very interested in my personal background: my family, where I grew up, my language facility; I'm fluent in Spanish as well as in English. I didn't think much of it at the time but when a white male got the job who was a Regional Sales Manager for three years less than me, I thought back on the interview with Stenton and got quite angry. I later heard through the grapevine that Stenton and the new Assistant Vice-President were members of the same club that doesn't admit anyone whose parents didn't come over on the Mayflower and I put two and two together.

(Pause - 10)

Q: In any of your previous promotions was your ethnicity considered in the way it was in this interview?

(Pause - 11)

A: Not to my knowledge. I'd received every promotion I applied for up until this one.

Q: So it wasn't, then?

(Pause - 12)

A: Right.

Q: So your ethnicity was never considered in previous promotion considerations, then?

(Pause - 13)

A: That's right. Those decisions were on the merits.

The direct examination of Rodriguez continued and was completed. We pick up the trial as the cross examination of Rodriguez begins.

Q: You have worked for BMI for fifteen years, haven't you?

A: Yes.

Q: During those fifteen years you have received four promotions?

A: Yes.

Q: You are 39 years old, correct?

A: Yes.

Q: That makes you the youngest Regional Sales Manager at BMI, isn't that right?

Q2: Objection, that assumes a fact not in evidence.

(Pause - 14)

Q: The man who received the promotion to Assistant Vice-President for Sales when you applied for that job was 45 years old at the time, right?

A: Yes, but I had more experience at BMI.

(Pause - 15)

Q: He was hired to work at BMI after a twenty-year career at RCA, wasn't he?

A: That's right.

Q: His last position at RCA which he held for eight years before joining BMI was the equivalent of your position, wasn't it?

(Pause - 16)

A: Roughly equivalent but not exactly so. My region is larger than his was at RCA.

Q2: Move to strike the last answer as non-responsive. The question could easily be answered yes or no.

(Pause - 17)

Q: So the person who got the job was older and had more experience than you, right?

(Pause - 18)

A: And he was a white male from the right club.

(Pause - 19)

Q: When you applied for this promotion, Ms. Rodriguez, you submitted a statement of why you were qualified for the Assistant Vice-President for Sales position, correct?

A: Yes.

Q: You mentioned how you worked your way through college and graduate school?

A: Yes.

Q: You wrote of growing up in a largely poor, Spanish-speaking neighborhood?

A: Yes, to show my ability to work hard for my goals.

Q: You also wrote of your being bilingual?

A: Yes, I believe that's an asset.

Q: All of these factors were mentioned by you, correct?

A: Yes.

Q: But when Mr. Stenton asked your about your personal and family background and the fact of your being bilingual he was discriminating against you, right?

(Pause - 20)

A: It was the way he asked--in a condescending way.

Q: Just a few more questions, Ms. Rodriguez. You have received four promotions at BMI, haven't you?

A: Yes.

Q: You've only applied for five promotions, correct?

A: Yes.

Q: Isn't it possible, Ms. Rodriguez, that this one time you just weren't qualified?

(Pause - 21)

Vignette 4

Patricia Jones was killed when the engine of a small boat in which she and her son were riding exploded. Her estate brought suit against the manufacturer of the boat and the designer of the engine. The defendants have denied liability, claiming that the engine exploded when hit by lightning. The plaintiff's first witness is Jason, son of the decedent. Jason is now six years old; he was four at the time of the explosion. We join the trial at the beginning of Jason's direct examination.

Q: Tell us your name.

A: Jason Jones.

Q: Where do you live?

A: Center City.

Q: Do you live on 8th Street?

(Pause - 1)

A: I don't know. I live in Center City.

Q: Jason, how old are you now?

A: Six.

Q: Can you count it on your fingers?

A: One, two, three, four, five, six.

Q: Jason, do you know where you are?

A: Yes.

Q: Where?

A: Court.

Q: Jason, do you know that if you don't tell the truth here today, bad things will happen to you?

(Pause - 2)

A: Yes.

Q: What is the difference between telling the truth and
    telling a lie?

A: Telling the truth is good; lying is not good.

Q: What does it mean to tell a lie?

A: It's when I don't tell my daddy something.

Q: Jason, I know this is hard, but I want you to think
    back to the day your mom died. Do you remember that
    day?

    (Pause - 3)

A: Yes.

Q: What's the difference between telling the truth and
    telling a lie?

A: The truth is real; a lie is when you make something
    up.

Q: What happens if you tell a lie?

A: My dad makes me go to my room.

Q: It's not good to tell a lie, is it?

    (Pause - 4)

A: No.

Judge: All right, counselor, let's go ahead and swear the
    witness.

    (Pause - 5)

Vignette 5

Last July, Jack Meade was killed in an auto accident while a passenger in Fred Haskell's car. The accident occurred on a rainy and foggy night. Evidently the car skidded off the road and ran into a tree, killing both Haskell and his passenger, Meade. Meade's estate brings a wrongful death action against Haskell's estate.

The plaintiff calls Rhonda Carter, a part-time auto mechanic, who was nearby at the time of the crash.

Q: Please state your name and address.

A: My name is Rhonda Carter and I live at Highway 47 in Centerville.

Q: How old are you?

A: 20.

Q: What do you do for a living?

A: I'm an auto mechanic.

Q: Directing your attention to 11:00 p.m. on the evening of July 14th of last year, where were you?

A: I was in bed reading.

Q: Where in the house is your bedroom located?

A: In the front left of the second floor, about 30 feet from the road.

Q: While reading at 11:00 p.m. on the night of July 14th, did you hear anything?

A: I heard a crash right in front of my house.

Q: After hearing the crash, what did you do?

A: I looked out the window and saw that a car had hit a big elm tree right in front of my house.

Q: Did you hear anything directly before
     the collision occurred?

A: Yes.

Q: What did you hear?

A: Well, I was sitting in bed reading and I
     heard this car on the highway. I heard
     the engine gunning--you know, really
     racing.

     (Pause - 1)

Q: Did you hear anything else?

A: Yes, I heard the tires squealing badly
     as if the car was out of control.

     (Pause - 2)

Q: Then what happened?

A: I heard the car smash against the tree
     with a loud crash.

Q: Based on everything you heard, how fast
     was the car going?

     (Pause - 3)

Vignette 6

Madeline Hart was kidnapped three years ago by a group of terrorists. Presently, she is on trial for the part she played in an armed robbery during the time she was kidnapped. Her defense is that she was coerced to commit the crime by her kidnappers.

In its case-in-chief, the prosecution produced a writing which stated that Madeline wished to overthrow capitalist society, and that she would rob a bank to accomplish this goal. The prosecution called a handwriting expert who testified that the incriminating statement was undoubtedly written by Madeline. To diminish the effect of the incriminating statement, the defense calls Dr. Margaret Singer, who claims to be an expert in the field of psycholinguistics.

Defense Counsel: Your Honor, at this time I would like to call Dr. Margaret Singer, whom we will qualify as an expert in the field of psycholinguistics.

Judge: Counsel, call Dr. Singer.

Defense Counsel: Thank you, your Honor.

Q: Please state your name and profession.

A: I am Dr. Margaret Singer, and I am a practicing psychologist.

Q: What is your educational background?

A: I received bachelors degrees in psychology and linguistics from Stanford University. I received a masters and a Ph.D. in psychology from the University of Michigan, where I was Magna Cum Laude.

Q: Are you a member of any professional
      societies?

A: Yes. I am a member of the American
      Psychological Association. I am a
      member of the league of Therapeutic
      Psychologists, and right now I am
      President of the National Society
      for the Study of Psycholinguistics.

Q: When did you become president of the
      Society?

A: Two years ago. I am one of the founding
      members.

Q: What is psycholinguistics?

A: Psycholinguistics is the study of how
      the human mind selects words for the
      purpose of expression. I and three
      other prominent psychologists
      formulated this theory around twelve
      years ago after extensive
      experimentation proved that every
      person has an idiosyncratic method of
      choosing words. By use of the
      accepted testing procedures in
      psycholinguistics, we can compare the
      normal word choice patterns of a
      client to another exemplar to
      determine if the exemplar was
      actually produced by the client in a
      voluntary way.

      (Pause - 1)

Vignette 7

The children of Marvin Dixon have brought a cause of action to set aside the December 25, YR-4 will of their deceased father that leaves the entirety of his estate to the Nita Humane Society. They seek to set aside the will on the ground that Mr. Dixon lacked the testamentary capacity to execute the will. The children call as a witness Dr. Joyce Martinez, a psychiatrist. We pick up in the midst of Dr. Martinez's testimony after she has completed stating her qualifications.

Q: Your Honor, I offer Dr. Martinez as an expert witness in the field of medicine with a specialization in psychiatry and ask that she be qualified to render an opinion as to the testamentary capacity of Mr. Marvin Dixon at the time that he executed the will in question in this case.

(Pause - 1)

Judge: Hearing no objection, she may be so qualified.

Q: Your Honor, will you take judicial notice that the legal definition for testamentary capacity is whether the testator had the mental ability to know what he was doing when he wrote the will, knew the effect of his acts in making the will, realized what he was doing, knew his relatives and knew the property he owned?

(Pause - 2)

Judge: That is the legal definition in Nita and I do take judicial notice of that definition.

Q: Dr. Martinez, are you aware of the legal definition of testamentary capacity as judicially noticed by the judge?

A: Yes.

Q: Dr. Martinez, have you come to an opinion as to whether Marvin Dixon possessed the testamentary capacity to execute a will as of December 25th YR-4?

(Pause - 3)

A: Yes, I have. In my opinion, Mr. Marvin Dixon did
     not possess the testamentary capacity to execute a
     will as of December 25, YR-4.

Q: On what do you base that opinion?

A: I have reviewed Mr. Dixon's medical records from
     the Nita Gerontology Center where he was living
     from January, YR-6 until his death on March 15,
     YR-1 and I have talked to a number of family
     members who were in contact with him during that
     period of time.

Q: Is this the type of information that you normally
     rely on in coming to an opinion such as the one
     you have given today?

     (Pause - 4)

A: It is not unusual in situations where I was not
     the treating physician to use such information,
     yes. Usually, the treating psychiatrist has
     better information because of personal interaction
     with the patient but in cases like this where the
     treating psychiatrist, Dr. Gordon, is deceased, I
     can use the information I referred to in coming to
     an opinion as to the mental state of a patient who
     I have not met personally.

     (Pause - 5)

Q: What do the medical records for Mr. Dixon show
     regarding his condition on December 24th and 25th,
     YR-4?

A: An orderly reports that Mr. Dixon became
     distressed on the evening of December 24, YR-4
     after watching an animated cartoon presentation of
     the poem "The Night Before Christmas." The
     orderly reports that Mr. Dixon seemed, and I'm
     using the orderly's words, "sad and depressed."
     The orderly also notes that Mr. Dixon had
     difficulty walking from the T.V. room to his
     bedroom and had to be helped into his bed.

     (Pause - 6)

Q: Is there anything else in the records for those
     dates?

A: Yes, Dr. Gordon notes in the record for December 25, YR-4 that Mr. Dixon became agitated and demanded to see his lawyer on Christmas morning. Apparently the lawyer came to see Mr. Dixon because Dr. Gordon reports that after being visited by a Ms. Carter, who I now know was Mr. Dixon's lawyer that he calmed down. Dr. Gordon wrote in the record that in her opinion Mr. Dixon, who was a manic depressive, apparently moved from a depressive state in the morning to a manic state in the afternoon.

(Pause - 7)

Q: What did you learn from Mr. Dixon's children?

A: Mary Dixon visited her father on Christmas morning and she told me that her father was quite anxious and appeared angry. She said that her father asked, "Who takes care of them the rest of the year?" with no apparent reference to anyone or anything.

(Pause - 8)

Q: Did any other of Mr. Dixon's children provide you with any information?

A: Yes, Marvin, Jr. visited his father on Christmas afternoon. During the visit his father was cheerful -- in his son's words, almost elated. Mr. Dixon, senior, told his son and his grandson who was also present not to worry about the reindeer, that he had taken care of them. Marvin, Jr. didn't know what his father meant but he did say that his son, Marvin III, seemed quite happy at the news.

(Pause - 9)

Q: What does all this mean, Dr. Martinez?

A: In my opinion, Mr. Davis became worried about the well-being of Santa's reindeer after watching the television animation of the poem, "The Night Before Christmas," called his lawyer the next day and changed his will to leave his estate to the Nita Humane Society to provide for their care.

(Pause - 10)

7.4

Vignette 8

The plaintiff, Acme Paper Company, has sued the Barton Fire and Casualty Company, the defendant, for payment pursuant to a fire insurance policy written by the defendant on the plaintiff's factory on 111 Main Street which was totally destroyed by fire on February 10th of last year. Barton defends, alleging that the fire was a result of arson by Jay Carlton, an employee of Acme, who set the fire at the behest of the owners of the Acme Paper Company. The parties stipulated that the fire occurred and that the Acme factory was completely destroyed. The burden of proof on arson is on the defendant. The defendant calls as its first witness Frank Grant, a Fire Marshal who investigated the fire. The parties have stipulated that Grant is an expert witness in the field of fire investigation and is qualified to give an opinion as to the cause of the fire. The direct examination of Grant continues.

Q: Were you on duty on February 10th of last year at about 10:00 p.m.?

A: Yes, I was called to investigate a fire at the Acme Paper Company at 111 Main Street.

Q: What did you do?

A: I talked to the firefighters who were at the scene, specifically to Donna Potter, who was the firefighter in charge.

Q: Why did you talk to her?

A: To get information necessary for my investigation.

Q: What did she tell you?

A: She said that the fire had spread very rapidly from the time she arrived on the scene at 9:00 p.m.

(Pause - 1)

Q. Did she tell you anything else?

A: Yes, she said that she took the call reporting the fire at 8:42 p.m. from a witness named George Jackson. Jackson told her that he saw flames coming out of the windows on the first, third and fifth floors of the building as he drove by at about 8:30 p.m.

(Pause - 2)

Q: What was the significance of Jackson's report?

A: His report showed that there were three separate and non-communicating fires at the same time, which is a strong indicator of arson. The recognized authority on fire investigations, Jane Byrne, says in her book <u>Fire Investigation</u> that where there are separate and non-communicating fires in a building, arson is indicated.

(Pause - 3)

Q: Is Ms. Byrne's book recognized by fire investigators as an authoritative text?

A: Yes, it's the bible for us.

Q: Your Honor, I ask that Byrne's book <u>Fire Investigation</u>, which has been marked as Defendant's Exhibit 1 for identification, be accepted in evidence and I request permission to publish Chapter 4, Section 12 of that book, which deals with separate and non-communicating fires, to the jury.

(Pause - 4)

The direct examination of Grant continued and he gave the opinion that the Acme fire was the result of arson. We pick up in the midst of the cross examination of Grant.

Q: You inspected the Acme building after the fire was put out, didn't you?

A: Yes.

Q: You found out that the electrical wiring for the first, third and fifth floors was all on the same circuit, isn't that right?

A: Yes.

Q: You discovered that there was faulty wiring in the circuit, didn't you?

A: Yes.

Q: That faulty wiring could have caused the fire, isn't that right?

A: It could have, but the result of all my investigation was that the fire was caused by arson.

(Pause - 5)

Q: Fire Marshal Grant, you referred to Jane Byrne's book, Fire Investigation, on direct examination, didn't you?

A: Yes.

Q: Ms. Byrne has a Ph.D. in chemistry, doesn't she?

A: Yes.

Q: And she's the chair of the Chemistry Department at City University, isn't she?

A: Yes.

Q: She's written over 100 articles on fire investigations, hasn't she?

A: Yes.

Q: In fact she wrote the book which you referred to as the bible, didn't she?

A: Yes.

Q: You've attended conferences where Dr. Byrne was the primary instructor, haven't you?

A: Yes, many times.

Q: Now Fire Marshal Grant, despite your qualifications, you wouldn't consider yourself as eminent an authority on fire investigations as Dr. Byrne, would you?

A: No, of course not.

Q: Let me show you Defendant's Exhibit 1 and refer you to Chapter 1, section 1. Doesn't it say there that, "The primary rule of fire investigation is that you should not reach the conclusion of arson unless and until you can rule out all accidental causes."?

       (Pause - 6)

A: Yes.

Q: Faulty wiring is an accidental cause, isn't it sir?

A: Yes.

Q: I have no further questions of this witness.

       The defendant's lawyer asked the following questions on redirect examination.

Q: Did you prepare a report of your investigation of the Acme fire at 111 Main Street on February 10th of last year?

       (Pause - 7)

A: Yes, I'm required as part of my duties as a Fire Marshal to file a report of all my investigations. The law in this state requires that I make my report within five days of completing my investigation.

Q: Showing you what's been marked as
     Defendant's Exhibit 2 for
     identification, do you recognize it?

A: Yes, that's my report on the Acme fire.

Q: Your Honor, I offer Defendant's Exhibit
     2 for identification in evidence.

Q2: We have no objection so long as the
     defendant's counsel will stipulate to
     the admissibility of the report of Dr.
     Morgan, whom the plaintiff will call as
     an expert witness during rebuttal.

     (Pause - 8)

<u>Vignette 9</u>

The defendant, Charles Rogers, a city police officer, has been charged with a murder committed while he was off-duty. The victim was shot dead-center in the heart. The defendant claims that his gun was fired accidentally while he struggled with the victim, who was the first aggressor.

The prosecutor calls the City Chief of Police as a witness.

Q: What is your name and occupation?

A: Joan Simmons, City Chief of Police.

Q: Do you know the defendant?

A: Yes, he's been on my force for seven years.

Q: What are his duties?

A: For the past two years he has been an instructor at our shooting range. He shows our new recruits how to accurately shoot at human silhouette targets. He does a good job.

Q: How was the defendant trained to shoot?

A: In the same way he now teaches the others.

Q: Is he a good shot?

A: He's an expert - the best we have.

Q: I see. When shooting at the silhouette, how does one obtain the maximum score?

A: It's done by hitting a circle drawn around the heart of the target.

(Pause - 1)

Vignette 10

The defendant, Robert Ryan, is charged with the murder of his wife after hearing his wife was leaving him for another man. His defense is insanity, disassociative reaction, which is characterized by amnesia regarding the traumatic events.

On cross examination of the defendant, the prosecution asks the following:

Q: Are you familiar with the book <u>Anatomy of a Murder</u>?

A: Yes, slightly.

Q: Have you read it?

A: I may have skimmed it.

Q: When was this?

A: It was a few weeks before my wife died.

Q: You recall, don't you, that in the book the defense asserted by the jealous husband charged with killing his wife was "disassociative reaction" which made him amnesiac?

A: I don't remember.

(Pause - 1)

On rebuttal the prosecutor calls the defendant's daughter as a witness. We pick up in the midst of the direct examination of Sarah Ryan by the prosecuting attorney.

Q: Are you familiar with the book <u>Anatomy of a Murder</u>?

A: Yes.

Q: Have you ever seen it in your
     parents' house?

A: Yes I did -- two weeks before the murder.

Q: Did you ever see anyone in the house
     reading this book?

A: Yes, my father.

Q: When did you first notice your father
     reading the book?

A: About two weeks before the murder.

Q: Did you ever see a bookmark in the book?

A: Yes, it was about two-thirds of the way
     into the book when I first saw my father
     reading it.

Q: And when did you last see him reading
     this book?

A: It would have been a week before the
     murder.

Q: Was there a bookmark in the book?

A: Yes.

Q: Where at this time was the bookmark
     placed?

A: It was about a fourth of the way through.

     (Pause - 2)

Vignette 11

Rick Jackson, an air-conditioning mechanic, is charged with importation and possession of marijuana. On May 1 of last year, Jackson and his wife arrived at Kennedy Airport in New York from Istanbul, Turkey. Customs officers found four pounds of marijuana in Jackson's baggage.

Jackson asserts that he is innocent. He claims that someone put the marijuana into his baggage, planning to recover it after the customs check. In effect, Jackson claims he was an unwitting courier. He claims that he and his wife were in Turkey as part of their lifetime dream: a second honeymoon.

The prosecution calls the police officer who made the initial arrest.

Q: Please state your name.

A: My name is Edna Hermann.

Q: Ms. Hermann, what is your occupation?

A: I have been a police officer for fifteen years.

Q: Officer Hermann, were you working on May 1 of last year?

A: Yes, I was.

Q: What happened on May 1?

A: I arrested the defendant on a narcotics charge in response to a call from the customs officers at Kennedy Airport.

Q: After arresting the defendant, what did you do?

A: I read the defendant his rights.

Q: Did you search the defendant?

A: Yes.

Q: Did you find anything?

A: Yes.

Q: What did you find?

A: The only thing he had in his pockets was a business card; you know, the kind they carry in wallets.

Q: Officer, showing you a card previously marked as Government's Exhibit #1 for identification, can you identify it?

A: Yes. It's the card I seized from the defendant.

Q: Your Honor, I offer this card as Government's Exhibit #1, and ask that the witness read it to the jury.

(Pause - 1)

A: The card says "Janet Samuels, Esq., 10 Court Street, N.Y., N.Y., phone number (212) 337-8707."

(Pause - 2)

Q: Do you know Ms. Samuels?

A: Yes. She is an attorney in Manhattan who specializes in criminal defense litigation - particularly drug cases.

Vignette 12

Porter, plaintiff, sues Stevenson, defendant, for personal injuries growing out of a barroom fight. In his case-in-chief, Porter called an eyewitness, Wills, who testified that the defendant struck the plaintiff in an unprovoked attack. Defendant's lawyer is now cross examining Wills.

Q: Mr. Wills, it's true, isn't it, that you knew the defendant Stevenson before the barroom altercation?

A: I guess I had run into him once or twice before.

Q: In fact, Mr. Wills, hadn't you attacked Mr. Stevenson in a fistfight approximately one year ago?

Q: Objection - this is a prior bad act which does not go to truth and veracity.

(Pause - 1)

Vignette 13

Bob Petry, the plaintiff, sues James Vitale, the defendant, for personal injuries arising out of an automobile collision. The plaintiff testified that the defendant ran a red light, causing the collision and his injuries, and rested. The defendant called a passenger in his car at the time of the collision, Jack Smith. Smith testified that the plaintiff, rather than the defendant, ran a red light, causing the accident. Petry now cross-examines Smith. We pick up in the midst of the plaintiff's cross examination of Smith.

Q: Mr. Smith, you knew the defendant, Mr. Vitale, before the automobile collision involved in this case, didn't you?

A: Yes.

Q: And you had worked for him for three years before the accident, hadn't you?

A: That's right.

Q: And about two weeks after the collision in this case you had an argument with the defendant because you were drinking beer on the job?

Q2: Objection - irrelevant.

Q: Your Honor, we'll connect this up in one or two more questions.

(Pause - 1)

Judge: The witness will answer the question.

A: Yes.

Q: It's true, isn't it Mr. Smith, that your boss, Mr. Vitale, told you that he wouldn't fire you for drinking on the job if you testified that the collision in this case was the plaintiff's fault?

(Pause - 2)

Vignette 14

David Hodkins, the plaintiff, has sued Business Machines Incorporated (BMI), claiming that he was fired from his job because of his age. The plaintiff was 50 years old at the time he was fired. The plaintiff calls Mary Laurenson, an employment counselor, to testify as to his damages. We pick up in the midst of the cross-examination of Laurenson by the defendant's counsel.

Q: Isn't it true that you were once employed by RCA in their Research and Development Department?

A: Yes, many years ago.

Q: Actually just four years ago, wasn't it?

A: I guess so.

Q: And weren't you fired by RCA for stealing and selling trade secrets?

(Pause - 1)

A: No.

Q: Let me show you what's been marked as Plaintiff's Exhibit #42 for identification. That's a letter you received from David Cartwright, the president of RCA, informing you that you were fired for stealing and selling RCA's trade secrets, isn't it?

(Pause - 2)

Q: Isn't it correct that you got caught at RCA because James Wheller of BMI informed RCA that you had attempted to sell RCA's trade secrets to BMI?

(Pause - 3)

Vignette 15

James Butler sues Don Green for assault and battery
growing out of bar fight. Green claims self-defense.
Butler calls Jane Davis as a witness to the fight, who
testified that Green attacked Butler. After so testifying
for the plaintiff, the defense cross examines.

Q: Ms. Davis, you knew the plaintiff before this
     matter arose, didn't you?

A: I guess so.

Q: In fact, you saw James Butler in another fight
     about six months earlier, didn't you?

Q2: Objection. Counsel can't impeach my client; he's
     not on the witness stand. Besides, this is a
     prior act which does not go to truthfulness. It's
     also prejudicial.

Q: Your Honor, if you allow me a few more questions,
     the relevance and admissibility of this line of
     questioning will become apparent.

Court: I'll allow a few more questions.

Q: Ms. Davis, you witnessed James Butler get into a
     fight about six months ago, didn't you?

A: Yes.

Q: That fight took place at Jimmy's Go Go Bar &
     Grill, didn't it?

A: That's right.

Q: And the fight happened because James Butler came
     to your defense when another man was annoying you,
     isn't that right?

Q2: I renew my objection, your Honor.

     (Pause - 1)

15.1

Vignette 16

Paula Price has sued Danielle Diaz for conversion of property. Price claims that when she left her ring for cleaning at Diaz's jewelry store it contained five high-quality diamonds, but when it was returned the diamonds had been replaced with glass. Diaz claims that the stones were glass when Price brought in the ring.

Paula Price is the first witness for the plaintiff. We pick up in the midst of her direct examination.

Q: Ms. Price, do you know other people who know the defendant, Ms. Diaz?

A: Yes, lots of my friends shop at her store.

Q: Have any of those people ever talked about whether Ms. Diaz is a truthful person or not?

A: Yes.

Q: Among those people, what is Ms. Diaz's reputation for truthfulness?

(Pause - 1)

Ms. Price concluded her direct testimony and there was no cross-examination. The plaintiff then called Gail Gibson. We pick up in the midst of Ms. Gibson's direct examination.

Q: Ms. Gibson, do you know the plaintiff, Paula Price?

A: Yes, I've known her since we were children.

Q: During the time that you have known her, have you formed an opinion about her character for truthfulness?

A: Yes, I have.

Q: What is that opinion?

(Pause - 2)

Q: Do you know people who also know the defendant, Ms. Diaz?

A: Yes, I do.

Q: In what circumstances do these people know Ms. Diaz?

A: Most of them have shopped in her store.

Q: Among these people, does Ms. Diaz have a reputation for honesty?

A: Yes, she does.

Q: What is that reputation?

(Pause - 3)

Ms. Gibson concluded her direct examination. We rejoin the trial at the beginning of her cross-examination by the defense.

Q: Ms. Gibson, you don't work, do you?

A: No, not right now.

Q: You used to work, though, didn't you?

A: Yes.

Q: Isn't it true you were fired from your last position as a cashier for stealing?

(Pause - 4)

Q: Isn't it true that your former boss accused you of stealing from the cash register?

(Pause - 5)

Q: And you in fact did steal from your employer's cash register, didn't you?

(Pause - 6)

A: No, I did not.

Q: No further questions.

This concluded the cross-examination of Ms. Gibson. Her re-direct examination by the plaintiff's attorney follows.

Q: Why is it that you are no longer working?

A: I've applied to return to school, to finish my degree. I'm fortunate enough that my family can support me while I finish my education.

Q: Getting back to the case at hand, had you ever seen Ms. Price's ring before she left it for cleaning at the defendant's jewelry store?

(Pause - 7)

The plaintiff concluded her case and rested. The defense called as its first witness the defendant, Danielle Diaz. We pick up in the midst of Ms. Diaz's direct examination.

Q: Ms. Diaz, do you know people who know the plaintiff, Paula Price?

A: Yes, I do. Lots of my customers are friends and business associates of hers.

Q: Among those people, does Ms. Price have a reputation for truthfulness?

A: Yes, I've heard people talk about her on many occasions.

Q: What is that reputation?

(Pause - 8)

A: She has a reputation as being a chronic liar.

Q: Do you know Gail Gibson?

A: Yes, we used to work at the same place. Neither of us works there anymore.

Q: Why doesn't Ms. Gibson work there anymore?

(Pause - 9)

Ms. Diaz concluded her testimony. The defense called as its next witness William Worker, an employee in Ms. Diaz's jewelry store. Worker testified that Ms. Diaz has a reputation as a truthful person and that Ms. Gibson has a reputation as an untruthful individual. We now pick up with the continuation of Mr. Worker's direct examination by defense counsel.

Q: Mr. Worker, you've just described to us how you have come to know the reputation of Ms. Price. Would you now tell us whether among that same group of people Ms. Price has a reputation for truthfulness?

A: I'll say.

Q: What is that reputation?

A: Not good; everyone says she'll say whatever she needs to say, whether it's true or not.

Mr. Worker concluded his direct testimony. We now pick up in the midst of his cross-examination by plaintiff's counsel.

Q: Mr. Worker, are you aware that Ms. Diaz lied under oath on an employment application?

(Pause - 10)

A: Yeah, but it doesn't change what I think of her.

Q: Mr. Worker, isn't it true that Ms. Price's diamonds were taken as part of a conspiracy between you and the defendant, Ms. Diaz, to substitute inexpensive glass for your customers' authentic gems?

(Pause - 11)

A: Absolutely not.

Vignette 17

Raymond Dawson is a criminal defendant on trial for Vehicular Homicide arising from his allegedly reckless driving of an automobile on January 1st of this year. The government's first witness, Ben Wilson, testified on direct as an eyewitness to Dawson's erratic driving at the time of the collision with the victim, who was a pedestrian.

On cross examination, defense counsel asks the following questions:

Q: Are you the same Ben Wilson convicted of assault and battery in Iowa three years ago for which you received an eighteen-month prison sentence?

(Pause - 1)

A: Yes.

Q: Weren't you also convicted of misdemeanor-assault in Minnesota last year?

(Pause - 2)

A: Yes.

Q: Didn't you also plead guilty in Minnesota six years ago for fraud for which you received a suspended sentence?

(Pause - 3)

A: Yes.

Q: Nothing further.

The defense calls the defendant Raymond Dawson to testify in his own behalf. Dawson denied driving recklessly on the night the victim died, claiming the victim caused the accident by running out in front of his car. On cross examination, the government asked the following question.

Q: Are you the same Raymond Dawson who was convicted
    in this state eight years ago of rape for which
    you received a sentence of four years in prison?

    (Pause - 4)

A: Yes.

Q: Weren't you also arrested for possession of stolen
    property just four weeks ago in this state?

    (Pause - 5)

A: Yes.

Q: Weren't you convicted of the misdemeanor of
    passing bad checks in this state three years ago
    for which you received a sentence of probation?

    (Pause - 6)

A: Yes.

Q: Weren't you also convicted of perjury in this
    state thirteen years ago, receiving a two-year
    sentence?

    (Pause - 7)

A: Yes.

Q: Now finally, Mr. Dawson, weren't you convicted of
    vehicular homicide and driving under the influence
    of alcohol in this state only last year, for which
    you received a three-year suspended sentence?

    (Pause - 8)

A: No.

Dan Johnson, a passenger in Dawson's car at the time of
the accident, was called by the defense and testified that
the victim ran out in front of Dawson's car. On cross
examination, Johnson was questioned only about his two-year-
old prior conviction for perjury, which he denied. After
Johnson was excused, the defendant rested and the following
occurred.

Q: (<u>Government's counsel</u>) Your Honor, by way of rebuttal I offer a certified copy, previously marked as D-1 for identification, of Dan Johnson's perjury conviction, as Defendant's Exhibit 1, and I would like the court's permission to publish it to the jury.

(Pause - 9)

Q: I now call Walter Winston to the stand as a rebuttal witness.

Q: Please state your name and address for the record.

A: Walt Winston, 533 Commonwealth Avenue in the city.

Q: What is your occupation, Mr. Winston?

A: I'm a bartender at Jonny's Bar and Grill in the city.

Q: Do you know Dan Johnson?

A: Yeah -- he comes in and drinks at my bar about twice a week.

Q: Directing your attention to January 2nd of this year -- were you working that day?

A: I was -- from 4:00 p.m. to midnight.

Q: Did you see Johnson on January 2nd?

A: Yes -- I definitely remember him coming into the bar and talking about his car accident on New Year's Day.

Q: What did he say?

A: He said that he and the plaintiff were in an accident on New Year's Day. He also said that Dawson had been drinking on New Year's Day and had run a stop sign, and struck and killed the victim who was crossing the street in the crosswalk.

(Pause - 10)

Vignette 18

Wayne Walker was waiting for a bus on the corner of Main Street and Kennedy Boulevard when two cars crashed in the intersection. A lawsuit was filed, with the plaintiff claiming that the defendant drove through a red light. The plaintiff's car, a Mercedes Benz, had been travelling northbound; the defendant's car, a Toyota, had been traveling westbound.

At the trial, the plaintiff testified and then called Walker to testify. Walker testified on direct examination that at the time of the collision the plaintiff, driving the Mercedes, had the green light. We pick up in the midst of Walker's cross-examination.

Q: Mr. Walker, this is not the first time you have answered questions about this accident, is it?

A: No.

Q: In fact, the very day after the accident someone came to your house and asked you questions, isn't that right?

A: Yeah, that's right.

Q: And you answered those questions, didn't you?

A: Yeah, I suppose so. I mean it wasn't formal questions like here in court, but I did tell the guy what I had seen.

Q: Your Honor, I have here a document previously marked Defendant's Exhibit "A" for identification. It is the statement of Mr. Walker given the day after the accident. I offer Defendant's Exhibit "A" in evidence.

(Pause - 1)

Q: Mr. Walker, isn't it true that on the day after the accident you told the investigator who came to your house that at the time of the collision the traffic light was green for the westbound traffic?

A: No, I didn't say that.

Q: Mr. Walker, please take a look at Defendant's Exhibit "A" for identification.

A: O.K., I've looked at it.

Q: That's your signature at the bottom of this document, isn't it?

A: Yeah, I signed it.

Q: And this is the document that the investigator filled out after he asked you questions about the collision, isn't it?

A: Yeah.

Q: I'm going to read from this Defendant's Exhibit "A," and I want you to tell me if I'm reading it correctly. Doesn't Defendant's Exhibit "A" say, "At the time of the collision, the traffic light was green for the westbound traffic?"

A: Yeah.

Q: And those words were on the page before you signed your name, weren't they?

A: Yeah, I suppose.

Q: Your Honor, I again offer Defendant's Exhibit "A" in evidence.

    (Pause - 2)

    Mr. Walker also admitted during cross-examination that three weeks prior to trial he had had dinner with the plaintiff's lawyer at La Bon Vie, the city's most expensive and exclusive French restaurant. We rejoin the trial in the midst of the plaintiff's redirect examination of Mr. Walker.

Q: Mr. Walker, when was the next time immediately before today that you and I spoke?

A: Yesterday, in your partner's office.

Q: What did we talk about?

A: What I could expect today.

Q: Did we talk about the collision?

A: Yeah, of course.

Q: What did you say about who had the green light at the time of the collision?

(Pause - 3)

Q: Mr. Walker, I'd like you to think back to the
     first time we met. Where was that?

A: In your office.

Q: And when was that?

A: About a week after the collision.

Q: How did you come to be in my office?

A: You asked me to come and make a formal statement
     of what I saw.

Q: Who was present?

A: You, me, and one of those stenographer people.

Q: What did you say about who had the green light at
     the time of the collision?

(Pause - 4)

A: I told you that the Mercedes had the green light.

Vignette 19

BMI sues Minicom in a contract action involving computer parts. The defendant, Minicom's Vice President for Purchasing, Michael Lubell, has testified on direct examination. We pick up in the midst of the cross examination of Michael Lubell. Refer to Vignette 36 for the factual background of this Vignette.

Q: Now Mr. Lubell, you testified on direct that you held four jobs prior to coming to Minicom, including a job as a computer programmer, isn't that correct?

A: Yes, that's right.

Q: Do you remember coming to my office for a deposition last July 12?

A: Yes, I guess so.

Q: Your lawyer, Mr. Richards, was there, wasn't he?

A: Yeah.

Q: You were under oath, weren't you?

A: Yes.

Q: I asked you some questions and you gave answers, correct?

A: Yes.

Q: I'm showing you a document marked as Plaintiff's Exhibit 22 for identification. That's your deposition, correct?

A: Yes.

Q: Directing your attention to page 8 of Exhibit 22, didn't I ask you the following questions and you gave the following answers: Question: "What jobs have you held before coming to Minicom? Answer: Shoe salesman, jeans shop operator, tie salesman. Question: Mr. Lubell, what other jobs have you had? Answer: None."

Q2:   Objection - beyond the scope of direct
       and irrelevant.

       (Pause - 1)

Vignette 20

Mark Berman, the plaintiff, has sued John Hunter, the defendant, for personal injuries that he sustained as a result of a car accident. The plaintiff has called as a witness Norman Harrison. Harrison testified that the defendant Hunter ran a red light and hit the plaintiff's car. Before cross examination begins, the defendant marks Harrison's deposition as Defendant's Exhibit 1 for identification and a statement allegedly made by Harrison to the defendant's insurance investigator, Ray Noll, as Defendant's Exhibit 2 for identification. The cross examination of Harrison begins.

Q: This accident happened on June 1st of last year, didn't it?

A: Yes, at 3:00 p.m.

Q: The police investigated the accident, didn't they?

A: Yes.

Q: You gave them your name and address?

A: Yes.

Q: On June 5th of last year you were visited at your home by Ray Noll, weren't you?

A: Yes, he came to my home.

Q: He told you he was investigating the accident of June 1st, correct?

A: Yes.

Q: You told Mr. Noll that you didn't see the accident happen, didn't you?

A: No, that's not true.

Q: Didn't you give him a signed statement to that effect?

A: No.

Q: Let me show you what's been marked as Defendant's Exhibit 2 for identification and direct your attention to the lower right-hand corner. That's your signature, isn't it?

A: No, it's not.

Q: Defendant's Exhibit 2 for identification isn't your statement?

A: No, it's not.

Q: You didn't write and sign Defendant's Exhibit 2 for identification saying that you didn't see the accident?

(Pause - 1)

Q: You did give a deposition concerning this accident on October 15th of last year, didn't you?

A: Yes.

Q: At that time you were under oath?

A: Yes.

Q: After you answered both my questions and the questions of the defendant's lawyer, those questions and answers were typed up, weren't they?

A: Yes.

Q: You read over your deposition and signed it, didn't you?

A: Yes.

Q: Showing you what's been marked as Defendant's Exhibit 1 for identification and directing your attention to the last page, that's your signature, isn't it?

A: Yes, this is my deposition.

Q: Directing your attention to page 22, line 8, I asked you how the accident happened, didn't I?

A: Yes, that's right.

Q: You responded, "I'm not really sure, but
     I think that the defendant ran the red
     light," isn't that correct?

A: Yes, but on reflection I am sure.

Q2: Your Honor, I ask that the jury be
     instructed that the deposition statement
     of Mr. Harrison not be considered for
     the truth of the matter asserted but
     only as a prior inconsistent statement.

     (Pause - 2)

     The defendant had no further questions on cross
examination and the plaintiff's lawyer asked the following
questions on redirect examination of the plaintiff's
witness, Harrison.

Q: At the time of your deposition did I ask
     you any questions?

A: Yes, after the defendant's lawyer.

Q: Directing your attention to page 52,
     line 6 of Defendant's Exhibit 1 for
     identification, please read the question
     and answer to the jury.

A: Sure, it says here, "Question: 'You told
     the defendant's lawyer that you weren't
     sure how the accident happened, what did
     you mean by that?' Answer: 'I'm not
     sure exactly what part of the defend-
     ant's car hit the plaintiff's car, but I
     am sure that the defendant ran the red
     light."

     (Pause - 3)

Q: Directing your attention to June 10th of
     last year at 5:00 p.m., where were you?

A: At your office to talk to you about the
     accident.

Q: Did I ask you how the accident happened?

A: Yes, I told you that the defendant ran
    the red light.

    (Pause - 4)

_____

    The plaintiff then testified as to his version of the
accident, stating that the defendant ran the red light and
also testified as to his injuries. The defendant cross exa-
mined the plaintiff. The plaintiff rested. The defendant
calls as his first witness Ray Noll. The direct examination
follows.

_____

Q: What is your name and occupation?

A: Ray Noll. I'm an accident investigator.

Q: Were you working on June 5th of last
    year?

A: Yes, I was investigating the accident
    between the plaintiff and the defendant.

Q: What did you do?

A: I obtained a copy of the police report
    of the accident and went to the home of
    one of the witnesses listed on the
    report, Norman Harrison.

Q: Was Mr. Harrison at home?

A: Yes, we talked briefly about the accident.

Q: What did he tell you?

A: He told me that he didn't see the acci-
    dent.

    (Pause - 5)

Q: What did you do after talking with Mr.
    Harrison?

A: I asked him if he would write out a
    statement that said what he told me.

Q: Did he do that?

A: Well, he said he was busy, so I asked him if I could leave my standard statement form for him to fill out so I could pick it up the next day. He agreed and I picked up the statement form from his spouse the next day.

Q: Showing you what's been marked as Defendant's Exhibit 2 for identification, do you recognize it?

A: Yes, it's the statement of Harrison that I picked up on June 6th of last year.

Q: Is Defendant's Exhibit 2 for identification in the same condition as when you received it from Mr. Harrison?

A: Yes, except I put my initials with the date on it when I picked it up.

Q: Your Honor, I offer Defendant's Exhibit 2 for identification into evidence.

(Pause - 6)

This concludes the direct examination of Mr. Noll. The cross examination by the plaintiff follows.

Q: You are not an independent investigator, are you sir?

A: No.

Q: In fact you work for the Acme Insurance Company, don't you?

A: That's right.

Q: You were working for Acme in June of last year, weren't you?

A: Yes.

Q: Acme had a policy on the defendant, John
     Hunter, in June of last year, didn't
     they?

Q2: Objection and I move for a mistrial.

     (Pause - 7)

Q: After this accident, you know that Mr.
     Hunter, the plaintiff, was dropped as an
     insured by Acme, don't you?

Q2: Objection and I move for a mistrial.

     (Pause - 8)

Q: You met with my client on June 8th of
     last year, didn't you?

A: Yes.

Q: You saw him at Memorial Hospital, didn't
     you?

A: Yes.

Q: At that time didn't you tell the plain-
     tiff that you had talked to the witness,
     Mr. Harrison?

A: Yes.

Q: Didn't you tell my client that in light
     of what Harrison said that you would
     write him a check, on the spot, for
     $15,000.00 and agree to pay all his
     medical bills if my client would sign a
     release?

     (Pause - 9)

Vignette 21

Plaintiffs are prisoners at Walpole State Prison. They bring an action against the state under 42 U.S. Code § 1983, a civil rights action, claiming that the prison conditions in the period YR-5 to YR-1 at Walpole violated the 8th Amendment to the federal constitution in that such conditions amounted to cruel and unusual punishment. In support of their allegations, the prisoners offered evidence that authorities provided no mental health treatment or facilities to the inmate population.

The plaintiffs call as a witness Douglas Jones, the warden at Walpole.

Q: Please tell us your name and occupation.

A: Douglas Jones, warden at Walpole State Prison.

Q: Warden Jones, did the prison provide any mental health facilities or treatment between YR-5 and YR-1 to the inmate population at Walpole?

A: No. We couldn't do it and maintain security.

Q: Did the prison provide such mental health and treatment facilities beginning January 1, YR-0.

     (Pause - 1)

A: Yes.

Vignette 22

The defendant, Harold Richardson, has been charged with the crime of the assault of Ron Reynolds. Richardson calls his neighbor, Robin Bartel, as his first witness. We pick up in the midst of Bartel's direct examination.

Q: Mr. Bartel, how long have you known the defendant, Harold Richardson?

A: About twelve years.

Q: How did you meet?

A: We have worked together for those twelve years at General Manufacturing Co. in Doylestown.

Q: Mr. Bartel, where does Harold Richardson live?

A: Jenkintown.

Q: And do you know Mr. Richardson's reputation for truthfulness in Jenkintown?

A: I do.

Q: What is that reputation?

(Pause - 1)

A: He is known as a truthful man.

Q: Mr. Bartel, do you have an opinion as to Harold Richardson's character for peacefulness?

A: Yes.

Q: What is that opinion?

A: He is a peaceful, gentle, man.

(Pause - 2)

Q: Can you cite any instance where Mr.
    Richardson demonstrated his peace-
    fulness?

    (Pause - 3)

The prosecution now is cross examining Bartel.

Q: Mr. Bartel, have you heard that the
    defendant Richardson beat up a woman
    named Jane Adams in Pennsylvania
    three years ago in a bar fight?

Q2: Objection - prejudicial and the plain-
    tiff is using specific instances of con-
    duct to impeach.

    (Pause - 4)

Vignette 23

Darlene Darrow is on trial for aggravated assault. The victim, Vicki Voight, never recovered from her injuries sufficiently to be called as a witness. The prosecution called as its first witness Fred Frank, a friend of the victim's and an eyewitness to the assault. We pick up in the midst of Frank's direct examination.

Q: Mr. Frank, how well did you know the victim at the time of the altercation?

A: Oh, gee, really well. We lived next door to each other all our lives and attended the same college. She had been dating my roommate for the two years before the fight. To answer your question, I'd say that at the time of the fight we had been close friends for twenty years or more.

Q: Do you have an opinion about Ms. Voight's character for peacefulness at the time of the altercation?

A: Yes, I do.

Q: What is that opinion?

(Pause - 1)

A: She was a very peaceful person.

Q: Mr. Frank, did you know the defendant before the date of the altercation?

A: Yes, I did.

Q: For how long?

A: For about three years. We worked together, and bowled in the same league.

Q: Had you formed an opinion about the defendant's character for peacefulness or violence, and again I want to you to address your answer to the time of the altercation.

A: Yes, I had.

Q: What was that opinion?

(Pause - 2)

A: That she is a violent woman.

The prosecution put on the remainder of its case and then rested. The defense began its case by calling the defendant. We pick up in the midst of the defendant's direct examination.

Q: Ms. Darrow, for how long had you known Vicki Voight before the night you and she got into an altercation?

A: I had known her for about three years. She was real good friends with Fred, and I worked with Fred. We socialized in the same circles a lot on weekends.

Q: Had you, at the time of the altercation, formed an opinion about Ms. Voight's character for truthfulness and honesty?

A: Yes, I had.

Q: What was that opinion?

(Pause - 3)

A: You couldn't depend on anything she said.

Q: Ms. Darrow, besides Mr. Frank, did you know other people who knew Ms. Voight?

A: Yeah, sure. Like I said, we ran in the same circles on weekends.

Q: Among the people you know, did you ever hear anyone discuss Ms. Voight with regard to how she interacts with people; that is, do you know her reputation for violence?

A: I sure did. Lots of people talked about her. She's got some reputation.

Q: What is that reputation?

(Pause - 4)

A: For as long as I'd known her, she was aggressive and violent.

(Pause - 5)

The defendant concluded her direct testimony. We pick up in the midst of her cross-examination.

Q: Ms. Darrow, isn't it true that just three months before the altercation with Ms.Voight you were involved in a bar fight with another patron of the bar?

     (Pause - 6)

The defense put on the remainder of its case and rested. On rebuttal, the prosecution called Robert Richardson. We pick up in the midst of Richardson's direct examination.

Q: Mr. Richardson, how long have you known Ms. Voight?

A: I've known Vicki for four years. We work together.

Q: Do you have an opinion about Ms. Voight's character for peacefulness?

A: I sure do. I remember in particular an incident that really solidified my opinion of her.

Q: Please tell us what happened.

     (Pause - 7)

Vignette 24

The estate of John Haynes brings a wrongful death action against Diane Doaks, allegedly arising out of a hit-and-run incident on August 11 of last year where Doaks killed Haynes, a pedestrian. The car involved was a brown Mercedes with a Pennsylvania tag number "ADH-418." Doaks does not own such a car. Haynes' estate calls Sgt. Wilson of the Pittsburgh Police Department. We pick up in the midst of Sgt. Wilson's testimony.

Q: Sgt. Wilson, do you know Ms. Doaks, the defendant?

A: Yes.

Q: When did you first see her?

A: Well, my partner and I were seated in a car in plainclothes in a parking garage in downtown Pittsburgh last August 11th at 4:00 a.m. We saw Ms. Doaks break into and steal a brown Mercedes 450 SL with the Pennsylvania tag "ADH-418."

Q2:   Objection - irrelevant and a prior bad act.

        (Pause - 1)

Vignette 25

At the trial of Ronald Davis for armed robbery while masked committed on August 6 of last year, the government calls as a witness Sam Walters, an owner of a firearms retail store. The government had earlier introduced a gun which was allegedly used in the robbery. We pick up in the midst of Walters' testimony.

Q: Mr. Walters, showing you Government's Exhibit #1 for identification, I ask you to inspect it. Can you identify it?

(After looking at it)

A: Yes, it is a .22 caliber pistol stolen from my store on August 1 of last year.

Q: How do you know?

A: Because the gun bears the serial number of the stolen gun.

Q: What happened in the robbery of the gun from your store on August 1 of last year?

Q2:   Objection, irrelevant.

Q: Your Honor, we'll connect this up in a very few questions.

      (Pause - 1)

Judge: He may answer.

A: Yes. A man entered my store at about 10:30 a.m. on August 1, brandished a knife and took this gun from a glass case in front of me.

Q: Do you see that man in court today?

A: Yes, over there - the defendant.

Q2:   Objection - this is a prior bad act offered on propensity. It's prejudicial.

      (Pause - 2)

Vignette 26

Richards sues Davidson for fraud, alleging misrepresentation in the sale of vacation land in Louisiana. The fraud involved the use of falsified photographs which misled Richards as to the nature of the land sold to him by Davidson. The photographs show dry, well-landscaped lots. The lots were actually marshland, ninety percent under water year-round. Richards calls Watson, the victim of an earlier alleged land fraud perpetrated by Davidson in Florida. We pick up in the midst of Watson's testimony.

Q: Mr. Watson, do you know the defendant, Richard Davidson?

A: Yes, I met him three years ago.

Q: How did you come to know him?

A: Davidson approached me about the sale of some vacation land in Florida.

Q: Did you talk with Davidson?

A: Yes, he offered to sell me ten acres of Florida land for $3,000 per acre and said the land was hilly and dry. He also showed me some pictures of what he said was the land.

Q: Do you have those pictures?

A: No, I threw them away last year.

Q: Can you describe the pictures?

A: Yes, they showed a green, hilly, dry area.

Q: Did you buy the land?

A: Yes.

Q: Did you ever visit it?

A: Yes.

Q: Describe what you saw.

A: It was flat bottomland which was mostly under water.

(Pause - 1)

Vignette 27

Peters sues Davidson in a defamation action. Peters alleges that Davidson told a number of people that Peters was "dishonest." Peters called Jones as a character witness and Jones testified that he had known Peters for 20 years and that, in his opinion, Peters was an honest man. We pick up in the midst of the cross-examination of Jones, the character witness.

Q: Mr. Jones, do you know that Mr. Peters
      was a party to a land fraud scheme com-
      mitted four years ago?

Q2:   Objection - irrelevant, prior bad act.

      (Pause - 1)

Q: Mr. Jones, are you aware that Mr. Peters
      pled guilty to perjury some twelve years
      ago in Pennsylvania?

Q2:   Objection - irrelevant and you can't
      impeach the plaintiff without a foun-
      dation on cross.

      (Pause - 2)

Q: Now you don't really believe that a per-
      son who perjures himself and defrauds
      people is "very honest," do you?

      (Pause - 3)

Vignette 28

Ralph Diamond is on trial for murder. Diamond calls a character witness, Rev. Thomas Nicholson. The direct examination of Reverend Nicholson follows.

Q: What is your name and occupation?

A: Tom Nicholson. I am a Methodist minister.

Q: Do you know Ralph Diamond, the defendant in this case?

A: Yes, I've known Ralph for fifteen years as a neighbor of mine.

Q: How often do you see Ralph Diamond?

A: Usually about once a month, around our apartment complex.

Q: Do you know how he spends most of his time?

A: He is rather reclusive, staying in his apartment. He does not work - he's on disability. His only real activity is to play pinochle with three other guys who come to his apartment.

Q: Do you know Mr. Diamond's reputation for peacefulness in the community?

A: Yes.

Q: What is it?

(Pause - 1)

A: He is known as a peaceful, gentle man.

Vignette 29

This is a libel action brought by Brian Peters against James Donnelly. According to the complaint, Donnelly called Peters a "damned liar" in response to a question from a third party who asked Donnelly about Peters.

Defendant Donnelly calls James Johnson as a witness. We pick up in the midst of Johnson's testimony.

Q: Mr. Johnson, do you know Brian Peters, the plaintiff in this case?

A: Yes, I do.

Q: How do you know him?

A: I am the personnel director at Bergen Advertising, where Mr. Peters worked up to a month ago and I interviewed and hired Peters for our art department.

Q: When you interviewed Peters, did he describe his educational background?

A: Yes - he said he was a graduate of the Rhode Island School of Design.

Q: Did you ever discuss Peters' college degree with him again?

A: Yes. After his six-month probationary period was over, he came to me and said he expected a negative evaluation from his supervisor, who was dissatisfied with his skills. He then admitted he was a self-taught artist and had no formal training at RISD or anywhere.

(Pause - 1)

Vignette 30

The defendant, Helen Hoover, a prominent public official, is on trial for using and possessing cocaine. In pretrial pleadings and in its opening statement, the defense placed its emphasis on a defense of entrapment. As its first witness, the prosecution calls Rex Ray, who cooperated with the government in its investigation of Hoover. We pick up in the midst of Ray's testimony.

Q: Mr. Ray, how long had you known Ms. Hoover before the day of her arrest?

A: For about three years; we met at a political function and became friends.

Q: What kinds of things did you do together?

A: In the beginning we would get together for an after-work drink or dinner; later we started doing drugs together.

Q: Objection, your Honor; I move to strike the last clause of the witness' answer. Unless and until Ms. Hoover testifies, she cannot be impeached with specific acts of conduct, and even then the acts must pertain to truthfulness or untruthfulness.

(Pause - 1)

The prosecution completed its case and rested. As its first witness the defense called the defendant, Helen Hoover. We pick up in the midst of Hoover's direct examination.

Q: Ms. Hoover, had you at any time before the night in question used any form of contraband drugs?

A: No, I never did. In fact, on several occasions people used drugs in my presence and even offered me some, but I always said no. Moreover, on a voluntary basis I and everyone in my office participate in random urinalysis. I would have never done that if I used drugs.

Q2: Objection, your Honor, I move to strike everything following the statement, "No, I never did." Everything else is self-serving description and outside the bounds of any permissible prior act evidence.

(Pause - 2)

The defendant concluded her direct examination. We join the trial in the midst of the defendant's cross-examination by the prosecution.

Q: Ms. Hoover, you admit that you used cocaine on the night of your arrest, don't you?

A: Yes, I admit it, but only because that rat, Reed, tricked me into it.

Q: But that wasn't the first time you used cocaine, was it?

Q2: Objection, your Honor. Cocaine use does not go to truth and veracity and as such cannot form the basis of specific act impeachment.

(Pause - 3)

Vignette 31

The plaintiff, John Newman, was fired from his job as a state employment counselor. Presently, he brings a lawsuit against the State alleging that he was unlawfully discharged due to his unconventional religious beliefs in direct contravention of the Governor's Guidelines for Employment Procedures. The State defends claiming that John was discharged because the State had cut its budget.

We join the trial now, while the plaintiff is on the witness stand testifying as to the events surrounding his discharge.

Q: Mr. Newman, are you familiar with the state's procedure for discharging its employees?

A: Yes, I am. All state employment practices are contained exclusively in the Governor's Guidelines for Employment Procedures.

Q: How is it that you are familiar with the Governor's Guidelines?

A: Well, as a state employment counselor I had to constantly refer to the Governor's Guidelines to inform people who sought advice.

Q: Are the Guidelines for discharging employees mandatory or merely suggested procedures?

(Pause - 1)

Q: Under the Governor's Guidelines are employees' personal beliefs allowed to be taken into account in discharge decisions?

(Pause - 2)

A: No, the Guidelines specifically prohibit personal beliefs to be considered.

31.1

Q: Is there any reason to believe that in
      your case your personal beliefs were
      considered?

A: Yes, the State Employment Commission
      sent a memorandum to Employment
      Counselors advising that State Employees
      would be fired if they actively believed
      in a cult religion.

Q: What exactly did this memorandum say?

      (Pause - 3)

Q: Turning to the administrative hearing on
      your discharge, are there written atten-
      dance records kept at these hearings?

A: Yes, there are.

Q: Do you remember who was there?

A: Yes.

Q: Who attended your hearing?

      (Pause - 4)

Vignette 32

Paul sues Daniels for breach of contract. Paul alleges Daniels failed to pay for floor tile sold under a written contract. We pick up in the midst of Paul's testimony.

Q: Mr. Paul, you have earlier testified that you and Daniels entered into a written agreement for the sale of the tile?

A: Yes.

Q: Do you have a copy of that agreement with you today?

A: No.

Q: Then, Mr. Paul, do you remember the terms of the agreement?

A: I do. I agreed to sell Daniels 14 boxes of floor tile at $1,000 per box.

(Pause - 1)

Q: Do you have the original of the contract?

A: No.

Q: Where is it?

A: My copy was destroyed in a fire at my plant.

Q: What did that contract provide?

(Pause - 2)

Q: Who else had a copy of the contract?

A: Mr. Daniels did.

Q: What did the contract say?

Q2: Objection, we never received a subpoena for our copy of the contract and the plaintiff has the burden of proof.

(Pause - 3)

    After Paul rested, Daniels put on his
case and called himself as a witness. We
pick up in the midst of Daniels'
testimony.

Q: Mr. Daniels, did you enter into any
      agreement with Mr. Paul to buy tiles?

A: Yes.

Q: Did you pay for the tiles?

A: Yes, $14,000 and I even got a receipt to
      prove it.

Q2:   Objection - original document rule.

      (Pause - 4)

Vignette 33

John Harrison, the owner of an Army surplus store, has sued one of his suppliers, David Martin, for failing to deliver to Harrison 100 gross army blankets for which Harrison claims they had a contract. Martin admits that he made a written offer to sell the blankets but contends that he did not receive Harrison's written acceptance within the time limit of the offer and therefore there was no contract. The plaintiff, Harrison, is on the stand and has testified that he received the defendant Martin's offer on September 1st of last year to sell him the 100 gross blankets for $45,000.00. The offer letter provided that Harrison had to respond in writing before October 1st. We pick up in the midst of the direct examination of Harrison.

Q: What did you do in response to Martin's offer?

A: I wrote a letter to him on September 20th.

Q: Showing you what's been marked as Plaintiff's Exhibit #2 for identification, do you recognize it?

A: Yes, that's the carbon copy of the letter that I sent to Martin.

Q: What happened to the original?

A: It was mailed to Martin.

Q: Do you actually remember mailing the letter?

A: No.

Q: Did your business have a regular procedure for mailing letters in September of last year?

A: Yes. After the letter is typed I read it over for errors, check the address to make sure it is correct both on the letter and the envelope, sign it and put the letter, the envelope and the copy in my out box. My secretary then folds the letter, runs the envelope through our postage meter and drops the letter in the postal slot outside our office. He then files the carbon in a file under the name of the addressee.

Q: When did you last see Plaintiff's Exhibit #2 for identification before you saw it in court today?

33.1

A: I took it out of our file on Martin before I came to court today.

Q: Your Honor, we made a request of the defendant to produce the original of Plaintiff's Exhibit #2 for identification and he has responded that he does not have it. We therefore offer Plaintiff's Exhibit #2 for identification into evidence.

(Pause - 1)

Vignette 34

We pick up in the midst of the plaintiff Parsons' testimony. Assume the same fact pattern as Vignette 2 of Parsons v. Dornan.

Q: Mr. Parsons, I show you a piece of paper that has been marked as Plaintiff's Exhibit 2. Do you recognize it?

A: Yes, it's a diagram of the intersection of 68th Street and Sherwood in the city.

Q: Did you make this diagram?

A: No.

Q: I offer this diagram in evidence as Plaintiff's Exhibit 2.

   (Pause - 1)

Vignette 35

Assume the same fact pattern as Vignette 2.

Q: Mr. Parsons, I show you this photograph previously marked as Plaintiff's #3 for identification. Can you tell us what it is?

A: Yes - a picture of the intersection of 68th and Sherwood Avenue.

Q: Who took this photograph?

A: I have no idea.

Q: Is it a fair and accurate representation of that intersection?

A: Yes.

Q: I move the admission of Plaintiff's #3 in evidence.

(Pause - 1)

Q2: I'd like a voir dire examination concerning the photograph, your Honor, prior to your ruling on its admission. I ask this be done outside the hearing of the jury.

(Pause - 2)

Voir Dire of Parsons

Q: Mr. Parsons, showing you Plaintiff's #3 for identification, do you see any traffic lights in that photograph?

A: Why - no.

Q: Indeed, do you see a stop sign at the Sherwood Avenue entrances to the intersection?

A: Yes.

Q: On the date of the accident there were
      traffic lights at the intersection of
      68th and Sherwood, weren't there.

A: Yes.

Q: Your honor, I object to the offer of
      Plaintiff's #3 as an exhibit.

      (Pause - 3)

Vignette 36

BMI, a giant corporation, is suing Minicom, a small company, for Minicom's failure to pay for three shipments of computer connector plugs which BMI claims it sold to Minicom. Minicom defends, claiming that the first shipment was late, the second shipment was the wrong part, and the third shipment was never received. BMI calls Chris Kay, its Regional Sales Manager, who BMI alleges negotiated the Minicom contracts. We pick up in the midst of Kay's testimony.

Q: Now, Mr. Kay, with respect to the first Minicom order which you have told us about, how did that sale come about?

A: Well, on January 12 of last year, Michael Lubell, the vice president for purchasing of Minicom, called me and placed an order for 3,500 BMI connector plugs at the price of $1.00 per plug.

(Pause 1)

Q: Mr. Kay, I show you an item previously marked as Plaintiff's Exhibit #1 for identification and I ask you what it is?

A: This is the page from my phone log dated January 12 of last year.

Q: Is there any entry on Plaintiff's Exhibit #1 for identification that refers to Minicom on that day?

A: Yes.

Q: What does the entry say?

(Pause - 2)

Q: Mr. Kay, directing your attention to the second Minicom order you mentioned earlier in your testimony, how was that order initiated?

A: I received a letter from Mike Lubell on January 16 of last year.

Q: Showing you a document previously marked
     as Plaintiff's Exhibit #2 for iden-
     tification, can you identify this docu-
     ment?

A: Yes, this is the letter from Lubell
     that I received at my office.

     (Pause - 3)

Q: Mr. Kay, after receiving Plaintiff's
     Exhibit #2 for identification, what did
     you do?

A   I spoke with my assistant, Virginia
     Young, and she sent a letter to
     Lubell accepting the second order.

     (Pause - 4)

Q: Mr. Kay, showing you a copy of a docu-
     ment previously marked as Plaintiff's #3
     for identification, can you identify it?

A: Yes, this is a Xerox of Ms. Young's
     letter to Lubell.

     (Pause - 5)

Q: Mr. Kay, directing your attention to the
     third BMI - Minicom transaction you men-
     tioned in your earlier testimony, how
     did this transaction begin?

A: On January 20 of last year, I called
     Minicom and left a message with Lubell's
     secretary inviting Lubell to a golfing
     weekend at Hilton Head, South Carolina
     on February 8th and 9th of last year.

     (Pause - 6)

Q: Did you go to Hilton Head?

A: Yes.

Q: Who else was there?

A: A lot of our newer customers, including
     Mr. Lubell and his wife.

Q: Did you have any conversation with
     Lubell?

A: Yes.

Q: Where?

A: In the clubhouse.

Q: Who else was there?

A: Just he and I.

Q: What did Lubell say to you?

A: He ordered 10,000 more interconnector
     plugs at $1.00 per plug for delivery
     within 14 days.

     (Pause - 7)

Q: Did you say anything?

A: Yes, I accepted the offer on the usual terms.

     After BMI rested, Minicom put in its case. Among other
defenses, Minicom's Michael Lubell denied he had been at
Hilton Head in February of last year and denied ever placing
the order attributed to him in the clubhouse conversation.
On rebuttal, BMI recalls Chris Kay to introduce a photograph
of Kay and Lubell which was allegedly taken at Hilton Head
on February 8th or 9th of last year.

Q: Your Honor, may the court reporter
     mark this as Plaintiff's #7 for
     identification and may I approach
     the witness?

Judge: Yes.

Q: Mr. Kay, I show you this photograph
     marked as Plaintiff's #7 for
     identification - can you identify it?

A: Yes, but I didn't take the photograph.
     The official Hilton Head photographer
     took it.

Q: What does Plaintiff's Exhibit #7 for
      identification show?

      (Pause - 8)

Vignette 37

The State has moved to involuntarily commit Richard Roe
for mental health treatment. In support of its claim that
Roe suffers from a mental disease or abnormality, the State
has called Dr. Jane Bonner, a psychiatrist, to testify
regarding her diagnosis. We pick up in the midst of Dr.
Bonner's testimony.

Q: Dr. Bonner, have you interviewed Mr. Roe?

A: Yes, on two occasions.

Q: Please tell the court when these meetings took
      place.

A: Three weeks ago - June 21st and 22nd, at the State
      Treatment Center.

Q: Please tell us how the first meeting began.

A: I introduced myself as Dr. Bonner.

Q: Did Mr. Roe respond?

A: Yes, he said: "I am the Emperor, Napoleon."

Q2:   Objection, hearsay.

      (Pause - 1)

Vignette 38

Dennis McClain has sued Alexander Barber for personal injuries arising from an automobile collision. James Patterson is an eyewitness to the collision. The plaintiff has called Patterson as a witness. We pick up in the midst of Patterson's direct examination.

Q: Mr. Patterson, did you ever discuss the automobile collision with anyone before coming to court?

A: Yes. I discussed it with some people at work.

Q: When was that?

A: About three weeks after it happened.

Q: What did you say?

Q2: Objection. Hearsay.

Q: Your Honor, I am offering a statement from a witness who is present in court, subject to cross examination. This isn't hearsay.

(Pause - 1)

Vignette 39

The Government charges David Polk, a garment factory owner, with knowingly hiring an illegal alien, Robert Alton. At trial, the Government calls Charles Wall, one of Polk's employees, as a witness. We pick up in the midst of Wall's testimony.

Q: Mr. Wall, as an employee of David Polk, what are your duties?

A: I work a sewing machine and supervise other sewing machine operators.

Q: Directing your attention to the morning of July 1 of last year, were you working that day?

A: Yes, I arrived at 8:30 a.m. as usual.

Q: When you arrived, what did you do?

A: I dropped by Mr. Polk's office and we talked. I told him that I had seen Bob Alton's immigration papers and that they were phony.

Q2: I object. This is hearsay. The Government can't prove Alton's an illegal alien with this out-of-court statement.

(Pause - 1)

Vignette 40

Mary Larson, the purchasing agent for a small radio manufacturer, Radiocom, Inc., called David Jones, Sales Manager for BMI, a large manufacturer of electronic parts, to place an order. Radiocom claims Larson placed an order and that BMI accepted it. When BMI failed to deliver, Radiocom sued for breach of contract. Radiocom calls Larson as a witness. We pick up in the midst of Larson's direct examination.

Q: Now Ms. Larson, do you know a person by the name of David Jones?

A: Yes, I do.

Q: Who is he?

A: He's the Sales Manager for BMI.

Q: When did you first meet him?

A: We met at a golf outing which BMI sponsored for prospective customers last September at a local country club.

Q: Did you speak with Jones at any time that day?

A: Yes, we spoke for about 45 minutes.

Q: Was anyone else present?

A: No.

Q: What did you say to Jones?

Q2: I object. Hearsay.

Q: (At sidebar) Your Honor, if permitted to answer, the witness will say that she ordered 100 gross transistors and that Jones agreed to deliver them for $100,000.

(Pause - 1)

Vignette 41

On the night of April 1st of last year, Charles Wood drove his car off the road into a tree, killing one of his passengers, Clint Bronson. Bronson's estate brings a wrongful death action against Wood alleging Wood's negligence. It has been stipulated that Wood was intoxicated at the time of the accident. His blood alcohol level was .18 percent. Wood defends on the basis that Bronson assumed the risk.

Burt Alcorn, a surviving passenger in Wood's car, was called by the plaintiff to explain the circumstances surrounding the accident. We pick up in the midst of Alcorn's cross-examination.

Q: Mr. Alcorn, you were with Mr. Wood and Mr. Bronson just before the accident, weren't you?

A: Yes.

Q: You were at Jimmy's Tavern, weren't you?

A: Yes, all three of us.

Q: You were drinking, weren't you?

A: Yes.

Q: All three of you were drinking, correct?

A: Yes.

Q: Isn't it true, Mr. Alcorn, that while you were at the bar, you came over to where Bronson was standing and said, "We better get going. Wood is driving and he's getting so drunk he might kill us all?"

      (Pause - 1)

A: Yes.

Q: You left the bar with Bronson and Wood, didn't you?

A: Yes.

41.1

Q: And you all got into Wood's car to go to
    a party?

A: Yes.

Q: Before the three of you got in the car,
    didn't Bronson have an argument with
    Wood?

A: Yes.

Q: Didn't Bronson say to Wood that Wood was
    too drunk to drive?

    (Pause - 2)

A: Yes.

Q: Didn't Wood respond that Bronson could
    get a cab if he was worried?

    (Pause - 3)

A: Yes.

Q: But Bronson still got in the car, right?

A: That's right.

Q: As you drove to the party, didn't Wood
    turn to Bronson and say, "See, I told
    you I could drive?"

    (Pause - 4)

A: Yes, that's when we ran off the road.

Vignette 42

The Government is trying Marilyn Adams for the murder of Jim Jefferson. The case is circumstantial, and a key in tying Adams to the killing is proof that the victim, Jefferson, was dead by 10:00 p.m. on August 1 of last year. Defendant calls Max Jefferson.

Q: Sir, what is your name and occupation?

A: Max Jefferson. I'm unemployed.

Q: Did you know the deceased victim, Jim Jefferson?

A: Yes, he was my brother.

Q: Directing your attention to the evening of August 1 of last year, where were you?

A: At home.

Q: Did you receive any phone calls that night?

A: Yes, one from my brother, Jim.

Q: What was the time of the phone call?

A: I don't remember.

Q: What did your brother say?

A: He said, "This is a great episode of L.A. Law, isn't it?"

Q: I ask the Court to take judicial notice of the fact that L.A. Law airs from 10:00 - 11:00 on Thursday evenings on channel three in Nita City.

     (Pause - 1)

Judge: I take judicial notice of that fact.

     (Pause - 2)

Vignette 43

At the trial of Arnold Johnson for the murder of John Williams on Thanksgiving night of last year at the victim's home at 2020 Main Street, the government calls Tom Smith as its first witness.

Q: What is your name and occupation?

A: Tom Smith. I'm a welder.

Q: Mr. Smith, do you know the defendant, Arnold Johnson?

A: Yes. We've known each other for years. We see each other about once a week.

Q: Did you see the defendant during the last week of last November?

A: Yes, I saw him on Thanksgiving day.

Q: Where did you see him?

A: We met at his house.

Q: Who was there?

A: Just Arnie, Tom Atkins, and I.

Q: Was there any conversation?

A: Atkins told Arnie he thought he knew who had beaten up Arnie's younger brother the day before and that it was John Williams.

      (Pause - 1)

Q: What did the defendant say?

      (Pause - 2)

A: He said he would "get Williams."

Q: Was there any other conversation?

       (Pause - 3)

A: The defendant asked me if I knew where
       he could find Williams, and I said he
       lives at 2020 Main Street.

       (Pause - 4)

Vignette 44

Last year, Jack Rickels and Jim Watson attended a cocktail party given by Bob Snow. At the party, Rickels told Snow to keep an eye on his silverware because Watson was likely to steal it.

Watson learned of this conversation and brought suit against Rickels for slander. Watson has called Bob Snow as a witness. We pick up in the midst of the direct examination of Snow.

Q: Mr. Snow, what did Rickels say to you?

A: He told me to keep an eye on my silverware because Watson was likely to steal it.

(Pause)

Q: What did you say?

A: I said, "I hear you, but I can hardly believe it."

(Pause - 1)

Q: What happened then?

A: I told Rickels that I had to tell my wife what he just said to me and left the conversation and walked over to where she was standing.

(Pause - 2)

Vignette 45

This is a trial of Joe Dolan for robbery of a U.S. Post Office. At trial, the government's first witness is Frank Ramierez, a U.S. Postal Service employee who was the immediate victim of the robbery.

Q: What is your name and occupation?

A: Frank Ramierez. I am a Postal Service employee. I work at the stamp counter at the Central post office in the city.

Q: Were you on duty on June 10 of last year at approximately 10:00 a.m.?

A: Yes.

Q: What time did you get in that day?

A: Nine in the morning.

Q: What did you do when you got to work?

A: I looked at the new "wanted" posters which had come in the night before. I check out the new posters every morning, first thing.

Q: Had any new ones arrived?

A: Yes, one that said: "Wanted for armed bank robbery, 'Joe Dolan,'" and it had Dolan's picture.

(Pause - 1)

Q: Directing your attention to 10:00 a.m., where were you?

A: At my stamp counter. I had just sold a batch of new commemorative stamps with Hank Aaron on them.

Q: What happened next?

A: A man who was a dead ringer for the pic-
     ture on the new "wanted" poster entered
     the post office, came up to me with a
     gun drawn and said, "Hand over all your
     money or I'll blow you away." I said:
     "You're Joe Dolan!" and I gave him the
     money.

     (Pause - 2)

Q: How did the robber react when you said,
     "You're Joe Dolan?"

     (Pause - 3)

A: He said, "So you know you better give me
     the money."

     (Pause - 4)

Q: Is the robber in this courtroom?

A: Yes, right over there.

Q: Let the record show that the witness has
     identified the defendant, Joe Dolan.

Vignette 46

The Capper Beer Corporation and its president, Roberta Capper, are on trial for alleged antitrust violations. The prosecution contends that Roberta Capper engaged in price-fixing negotiations with Jack Rollins, president of the Rollins Beer Corporation. Neither Mr. Rollins nor his company has been indicted.

In its case-in-chief against Roberta Capper, the prosecution has called Capper's former secretary, Ronald Janko, to testify as to the events surrounding the price-fixing negotiations. We pick up in the midst of Janko's testimony.

Q: Mr. Janko, describe your duties when you worked as Ms. Capper's secretary.

A: I answered her phone and typed her correspondence. I also placed outgoing calls for her.

Q: Mr. Janko, showing you what has been marked as Government's Exhibit #1 for identification, can you identify it?

A: Yes, this is a letter I typed for Ms. Capper last May.

Q: Do you recognize the signature?

A: Yes, it's Ms. Capper's.

Q: Your Honor, I offer this letter as Government's Exhibit #1.

Q2: Your Honor, may we approach the bench?

Judge: You may.

Q2: Your Honor, we object to this letter as hearsay.

Judge: Let's see - the letter is from Roberta Capper to Jack Rollins of the Rollins Beer Corporation. It says: "Dear Jack - We intend to hold the price of our six-pack to $3.75 for the next twelve months. What's your position? Sincerely, Roberta Capper."

(Pause - 1)

Q: Mr. Janko, while you were typing this letter, were you alone?

A: No, Jim Jackson, our national sales manager, was waiting to see Ms. Capper and he was looking over my shoulder as I typed the letter.

Q: Did he say anything to you?

A: Yes.

Q: What?

A: He said, "I'm glad that Capper finally has acted on my negotiations with Rollins."

(Pause - 2)

Q: Mr. Janko, do you know Jack Bush?

A: Yes, he's the former vice president of our company.

Q: When did you last see him?

A: About three days after I typed this letter here.

Q: When you say "this letter" do you mean Government's Exhibit #1?

A: Yes.

Q: What were the circumstances of your meeting Mr. Bush that day?

A: The day after I sent the letter to Rollins Beer, Bush came in to see Ms. Capper.

Q: Did they have a conversation?

A: Yes, right in my office.

Q: What did Mr. Bush say?

A: Mr. Bush had heard about the price-fixing and he was real mad. He accused

Capper of breaking the law by fixing prices.

(Pause - 3)

Q: What did Capper do?

A: Ms. Capper didn't say anything. She just nodded her head up and down and smiled.

(Pause - 4)

Q: Did you discuss this letter with Ms. Capper?

A: Yes, after I was approached by the FBI I told her the feds were looking into Capper's pricing.

(Pause - 5)

Q: How did Ms. Capper react when she found out that there was a federal investigation of Capper Beer and price-fixing?

A: She panicked.

Q: Could you explain?

A: Well, when she found out about the investigation she asked me to gather up the Rollins correspondence files. Then we both went down to the paper shredder and we spent the afternoon shredding documents.

(Pause - 6)

Q: Mr. Janko, do you know if Mr. Rollins of Rollins Beer ever received Ms. Capper's letter?

A: Yes, he got it.

Q: How do you know that?

A: Well, I called him and asked him if he had received it. I know his voice from talking to him many times before on the phone and in person. He said he had gotten it.

Q: Did he say anything else?

A: Yes. He said that he would like to make
     a few changes in the agreement, but that
     $3.75 was a good price to set for the
     product.

     (Pause - 7)

Q: Was there any other conversation?

A: Yes, Mr. Rollins said that he intended
     to meet with Ms. Capper the next day to
     finalize the agreement.

Q: Anything else?

A: Yes. Rollins said that he had been very
     happy with the previous agreements with
     Ms. Capper and hoped this one would work
     out as well.

     (Pause - 8)

Vignette 47

James Mitchell and two co-defendants, Martin Jones and
Charles "Lefty" Smith, are on trial for armed robbery of a
bank. For purposes of this vignette, assume that you are
the defense counsel for Mitchell only.

Q: What is your name and occupation?

A: Bobby Crocker, detective with the City
      police department.

Q: Directing your attention to the morning
      of April 18 of last year, where were you
      that morning?

A: In response to a radio call that said
      there was a robbery in progress, I went
      to the Second National Bank at 5th
      Avenue and 42nd Street.

      (Pause - 1)

Q: When you got there, what did you see?

A: I saw three men leave the bank and jump
      into a waiting car.

Q: Are those men in the courtroom today?

A: Yes, right over there.

Q: Let the record show that the witness has
      identified the defendants, James
      Mitchell, Martin Jones, and Charles
      Smith.

Q: What did you do after the defendants got
      into the car?

A: I pursued them in my car for a few
      blocks until it ran into an embankment
      and stopped.

Q: What happened next?

A: Lefty Smith jumped out and yelled to the
      others, "Scatter. I'll take the money."

      (Pause - 2)

Q: Was there any other conversation?

A: Yes. As Marty Jones jumped out of the
     car, he yelled to Mitchell: "Damn it,
     Jim, when you got us together to plan
     this job, you said it was foolproof."

(Pause - 3)

Q: Then what happened?

A: I ran after Lefty Smith, the guy who
     took the money and I caught him. Before
     I could even give him the <u>Miranda</u> war-
     nings, he said: "I didn't want to rob
     the bank, but the other guys made me."

(Pause - 4)

Vignette 48

The defendant, Bob Bram, is on trial for the murder of Bill Darwin. At trial, the government calls the arresting officer.

Q: What is your name and occupation?

A: I am James Kelly. I am a City Police detective-sergeant attached to homicide.

Q: Were you on duty on the evening of April 20 of last year at about 10:00 p.m.?

A: Yes.

Q: What were you doing at that time?

A: I arrested the defendant here, Bob Bram, outside a bar on Halstead Street and gave him his <u>Miranda</u> warnings.

Q: Was anyone else present?

A: Yes, a woman named Nancy Moore.

Q: Did Nancy Moore say anything to you in the presence of the defendant?

   (Pause - 1)

A: Yes, she said she had seen the defendant having an argument with Bill Darwin, the victim, inside the bar fifteen minutes before the shooting.

Vignette 49

Jane Jackson sues John Drake for trespassing. The plaintiff has called Bob Jackson as its first witness.

Q: What is your name and address?

A: Bob Jackson, 10 Main Street.

Q: Directing your attention to the evening of July 18 of last year, where were you?

A: At home.

Q: Did you receive any telephone calls?

A: Yes, one.

Q: Who was it?

A: My sister, Jane.

Q: What did she say?

A: She told me she could see a man lurking in the garden outside her window. She said he'd been there for a couple of minutes.

   (Pause - 1)

Q: What did you say?

   (Pause - 2)

A: I asked who it was. She said, "It looks like John Drake." Then she hung up.

   (Pause - 3)

Q: What did you do?

A: I called back about fifteen minutes later and got her back on the line and I asked her "What happened?"

Q: What did she say?

A: She said she had gone outside right
      after our earlier phone call and had
      seen tracks of a man's shoes in the gar-
      den.

      (Pause - 4)

Q: Did she say anything else?

A: Yes, she said she heard a voice she
      recognized as Drake's nearby saying,
      "Let's beat it."

      (Pause - 5)

Vignette 50

Janet Thacker sues Mary Perone and John Stiller for assault and battery. Ms. Thacker was found unconscious with severe head injuries after having been brutally beaten. She immediately underwent a complex brain operation and was in a coma for seven days. When she finally regained consciousness, Ms. Thacker spoke with her brother, Steven, about the attack.

The plaintiff has called Steven Thacker to relate his conversation with his sister. We pick up in the midst of the direct examination of Mr. Thacker.

Q: Mr. Thacker, what happened on the seventh day after Janet's operation?

A: Well, she came out of her coma while I was sitting there and was able to speak.

Q: Who was in the room with her when she awoke?

A: Just me. It was late at night and everyone else had gone home.

Q: Did you call a doctor?

A: Not immediately. I wanted to talk to her first.

Q: What happened when she woke up?

A: She said "Please stop hitting me, Mary. What did I ever do to you?"

(Pause - 1)

Q: Then what happened?

A: Well, I walked over to her and showed her a picture of the defendant, John Stiller, that the police had left in the room. They told me that they thought Stiller was one of Janet's attackers.

(Pause - 2)

Q: What happened?

A: The second she saw the picture she began
     to scream and cry. She kept on saying,
     "It's him! He tried to kill me!"

     (Pause - 3)

Vignette 51

Vincent Baker sues the Veterans' Administration and Frances Knight, a former nurse at a V.A. Hospital. Mr. Baker alleges that he suffered physical harm because Ms. Knight poisoned Baker's food when he was a patient in the V.A. Hospital.

The plaintiff calls his treating physician, who first discovered the poison. We pick up in the midst of the doctor's testimony.

Q: Did you see the victim on April 1 of last year?

A: Yes.

Q: When did you first see him?

A: He was the first person I saw on my nightly rounds. I saw him at 6:30 - right after dinner.

Q: What happened when you saw him?

A: I asked him how he was feeling. He said he was feeling bad. So I checked his pulse and saw that it was extraordinarily slow.

(Pause - 1)

Q: Then what happened?

A: Well, I became concerned. I asked him when he began to feel badly. He said he began to feel bad right after dinner.

(Pause - 2)

Q: What did you do then?

A: Well, I looked at the remaining food on his dinner tray. The food had a small amount of a white, powdery substance on it. I thought it was poison.

Q: What happened then?

A: I asked him who had brought him his
dinner tray.

Q: What did the patient say?

(Pause - 3)

A: He said that Frances Knight had brought
in his dinner tray.

Vignette 52

Jon Baker, the Executive Director of REPAC, a local antipoverty agency, has been indicted on charges of illegally diverting federal funds from the agency to his own use. At Baker's trial, the government seeks to offer records kept by the agency of its receipts and expenditures. The government calls Robert Richardson, an accountant, as its first witness.

Q: What is your name and occupation?

A: Robert Richardson. I am a certified public accountant.

Q: Mr. Richardson, are you familiar with an agency called REPAC?

A: Yes, I had a contract to do their books and oversee its non-profit status for the past two years.

Q: Mr. Richardson, I show you this ledger book that's been marked as Government's Exhibit 1 for identification and ask you if you can identify it.

A: Yes, it is REPAC's financial ledger for the past two years.

Q: Mr. Richardson, do you know how Government's Exhibit 1 for identification is made and kept?

A: Yes, the ledger is kept in my office and I make entries in those books whenever I receive a call from either the defendant, Mr. Baker, or his deputy director. If they tell me that funds were received, I make the relevant entry with amount and date. If they tell me money was disbursed, I make the appropriate entry. I did this for the last two years.

Q: Your Honor, I offer Government's Exhibit 1 for identification as Government's Exhibit 1.

Vignette 53

The defendant, Jackie Carney, is on trial for armed bank robbery and felony murder. The prosecution has called police desk captain Frank Cannon who is in charge of all desk officers at the city police department. We pick up in the midst of the direct examination of Cannon.

Q: Captain Cannon, as desk captain, what are your duties?

A: Well, I supervise the desk officers who receive calls and write up crime reports.

Q: Is there a standard procedure for filing crime reports?

A: Yes, I set up the procedures myself.

Q: What are those procedures?

A: Well, the investigating officer is required to call the desk from the scene of the crime. He dictates his report over the phone. The desk officer will type up the report as it is given over the phone.

Q: Is this the procedure for bank robberies?

A: Yes.

Q: Do you recognize this sheet of paper which has been marked as Government's Exhibit 1 for identification?

A: Yes. This is a crime report written by officer Davis on April 1 of last year. I recognize his handwriting.

Q: Who is Officer Davis?

A: He is the senior desk officer.

Q: What does the Government's Exhibit 1 for identification refer to?

A: It says: "First National Bank Robbery -- Initial Crime Report."

Q: Who telephoned the report in?

A: Officer Harry Callahan. He's been on the force for five years.

Q: Does Davis know Callahan?

A: Yes, they're cousins.

Q: I offer Government's Exhibit 1 for identification in evidence.

(Pause - 1)

Q: What does Government's Exhibit 1 say?

A: It says: "Officer Callahan called in at 10:30 a.m. He reports the following:

1. He notes that the inside of the bank is riddled with bullet holes.

(Pause - 2)

2. Officer Callahan spoke with an eyewitness who was mortally wounded during the robbery. The witness said that Jackie Carney shot him. Callahan warned the witness that he shouldn't talk because he was going to die, but the witness kept talking.

(Pause - 3)

3. Officer Callahan reports that a bank teller has estimated that the robber took $17,000."

Vignette 54

Plaintiff, Pomeroy, sues defendant, Mutual Insurance, for failure to pay on a fire insurance policy when plaintiff's store was destroyed by fire. The defendant calls a police officer to the stand.

Q: What is your name and occupation?

A: Robert Daley. I'm a city police officer.

Q: Directing your attention to the evening of last February 1st, were you on duty that night?

A: Yes, and I responded to a call about a fire at the plaintiff's store.

Q: When did you arrive at the scene?

A: About 11:00 p.m.

Q: What did you see?

A: The store was burning out of control.

Q: Did you talk to anyone there?

A: Yes, I spoke to a firefighter.

Q: Did you make a report of that conversation?

A: Yes. I filled out an incident report that included his statement when I took a break about fifteen minutes later. I'm required to make and file a report as to all my investigations.

Q: Do you have the report with you?

A: Yes.

Q: Your Honor, I offer this report pre-
     viously marked as Plaintiff's Exhibit #1
     for identification in evidence as
     Plaintiff's Exhibit #1.

Judge: Admitted, if there's no objection.

Q: Would you read the firefighter's state-
     ment in your report to the jury?

A: It says: "Firefighter James Smith said:
     'I found three empty gasoline cans, some
     lighter fluid and homemade torches near
     the point of origin of the fire. There
     is no question the fire was arson.'"

     (Pause - 1)

Q: As part of your investigation, did you
     talk to anyone else?

A: Yes, a bystander named Laura Wilson.

Q: Did you make a report of that conversation?

A: Yes, in the same report.

Q: Please read it to the jury.

     (Pause - 2)

A: "Laura Wilson of 215 Elm Street said she
     was parked in her car across the street
     from the subject store just before the
     fire broke out and she saw a man running
     out of the store carrying a gasoline
     can."

Vignette 55

This is a trial in a tort action for negligence brought by David Smith against the Jones Moving Company. Smith claims that the movers damaged a number of items of personal property in moving Smith's household goods. Jones Moving Company's attorney has called Nick Strong, one of the Jones Moving Company's employees who actually performed the move.

Q: What is your name and occupation?

A: Nick Strong. I'm a truck driver and laborer for the Jones Moving Company.

Q: Directing your attention to September 1st of last year, did you have any jobs that day?

A: Yes, we moved Mr. Smith's stuff.

Q: Were any of Mr. Smith's items damaged?

A: Yes, I believe a few were.

Q: Do you remember what those items were?

A: No way, I've done a hundred jobs since then.

Q: Mr. Strong, I show you this document, previously marked as Defendant's Exhibit #3 for identification. Can you identify it?

A: Yes, it's a list of Smith's items damaged in the move.

Q: Did you make the list?

A: No.

Q: Who did?

A: John Weak, who was working with me that day. I watched him write it.

Q: Did you inspect the items on the list
     after Mr. Weak wrote it up?

A: Yes.

Q: When was the list made?

A: About an hour and a half after we left
     Smith's house and got back to our ware-
     house.

Q: Do you know today whether the list was
     accurate when it was made?

A: I can't actually remember, but I take
     these lists very seriously whenever I
     make them because they are often the
     subjects of lawsuits.

Q: Your Honor, I offer this list into evi-
     dence as Defendant's Exhibit #3 for
     identification into evidence.

     (Pause - 1)

Q: Were there any additional items of
     Smith's damaged?

A: Yes, I think so.

Q: Can you remember what they were?

A: No way.

Q: Now I show you this document previously
     marked as Defendant's Exhibit #4. Can
     you identify it?

A: Yeah, this is a supplementary list of
     Smith's damaged items.

Q: Who made it and when?

A: Weak made this a day after the move. I
     recognize his handwriting. I went to
     Smith's house by myself and looked at
     the items. I then called Weak on the
     phone at the office and told him about
     the twelve additional damaged items and
     I told him to write down these items on
     the list.

Q: Your Honor, I offer Defendant's Exhibit
     #4 for identification in evidence.

     (Pause - 2)

_____

     The defendant-mover now calls John Weak.   We pick up in
the midst of Weak's testimony.

_____

Q: Mr. Weak, were you working on the day
     after David Smith's move?

A: Yes.

Q: Where?

A: I was in the office all day.

Q: Did you receive any phone calls that day?

A: Yes.

Q: Do you remember the names of any one of
     those callers?

A: Well, I remember that Nick Strong called
     in saying he was calling from Smith's
     new house and named about a dozen
     damaged items.

Q: What did you do when Nick named the
     items?

A: When he named each one, I wrote it down
     on a list.

Q: Then what action did you take?

A: I read each item back to Nick right
     after putting it on the list to make
     sure I had it right.

Q: Mr. Weak, do you know today that the
     list was accurate when it was made?

A: Yes -- I always take great care in
     keeping track of customer damage
     complaints.

Q: Mr. Weak, showing you a document pre-
     viously marked as Defendant's Exhibit 4
     for identification, can you identify it?

A: Yes, this is the list I just described
     of Smith's damaged furniture -- the list
     I took over the phone from Nick Strong.

Q: Your Honor, I offer Defendant's Exhibit
     4 for identification in evidence.

     (Pause - 3)

Vignette 56

Peters has brought an action for personal injuries and property damage to his automobile against National Foods Corporation, growing out of an accident in which a National Foods truck rear-ended Peters' automobile.

At the trial Davis, the defendant, calls John Jones, an employee of National Foods.

Q: Please tell us your name and occupation.

A: I am John Jones and I am employed by National Foods. I'm in charge of investigating claims, including those growing out of auto accidents, made against National or its employees while on the job.

Q: When an automobile accident involving National is reported to you, what do you do?

A: I go out and investigate the damage and cause of the accident and then write up and file a report which is maintained in the company's permanent files.

Q: How many of these reports have been filed in the last twelve months?

A: About seventy-five.

Q: Who did the report on the accident involved in this case?

A: I did.

Q: I show you a document marked as Defendant's Exhibit #1 for identification and ask you if you recognize it.

A: Yes, this is the report of the accident in this case.

Q: Your Honor, I offer Defendant's Exhibit #1 for identification as Defendant's Exhibit #1.

   (Pause - 1)

Vignette 57

The trial of the case of <u>Acme Paper Company v. Barton Fire and Casualty Company</u> continues. (See Vignette 8.) The defendant calls as a witness Georgia Meredith, who was the accountant and business consultant for Acme Paper Company until February 10th of last year, the day of the fire. The direct examination of Meredith follows. The parties have stipulated that Meredith is an expert in the field of accounting.

Q: What is your name and profession?

A: My name is Georgia Meredith. I am a Certified Public Accountant and I operate the Meredith Accounting and Business Consulting Company. I do regular accounting work as well as advising clients on general business matters.

Q: Have you ever done business with Acme Paper Company?

A: Yes, they were one of my clients until February 10th of last year when their factory burned down.

Q: What did you do for them?

A: I maintained their books and advised them as to business matters.

Q: Did you prepare an analysis of the financial condition of the Acme Paper Company as of February 10th of last year.

A: Yes, I did.

Q: How did you go about doing that?

A: I reviewed the books and records of Acme Paper Company and, applying generally accepted accounting techniques, came to a conclusion as to the net worth of the Company.

Q: Did you prepare a report of your conclu-
sions?

A: Yes. It is an amalgamation of all the
books and records of the Acme Paper
Company for the past five years.

Q: Showing you what's been marked as
Defendant's Exhibit #5 for identification
do you recognize it?

A: Yes, that's the report I just testified
about.

Q: Your Honor, I offer Defendant's Exhibit
#5 for identification in evidence.

(Pause - 1)

Assume that the financial status report for Acme Paper
Company shows that the company lost 2.3 million dollars over
the five years before the fire. The direct examination of
Ms. Meredith continues.

Q: What sorts of business advice did you
provide to Acme Paper Company?

A: I would advise them as to new areas of
business and on how to increase their
current business.

Q: Did you refer to any materials in giving
this advice?

A: Yes.

Q: What materials were they?

A: For the most part I used the reports of
the American Paper Institute which is the
paper industry watch dog for business
trends and the like.

Q: Do you know what the trends in the paper industry were in the past two years before the Acme fire?

A: Yes, the paper industry was in general decline and the prospects for last year and this year were not good.

Q: Showing you what's been marked as Defendant's Exhibit #6 for identification, do you recognize it?

A: Yes, it's the January report of the American Paper Institute for last year. I gave a copy of the report to Acme in January of last year.

Q: Your Honor, I offer Defendant's Exhibit #6 for identification in evidence.

(Pause - 2)

_____

That concludes the direct examination of Ms. Meredith. The cross-examination follows:

_____

Q: Ms. Meredith, isn't it a fact that your employment with the Acme Paper Company ended on February 10th of last year?

A: Yes, there was the fire.

Q: Weren't you actually terminated by Martin Anderson, the President of Acme, on the day of February 10th, before the fire happened?

A: Well, we agreed that given the condition of the company that my services could no longer be afforded by them.

Q: Isn't February the 10th of last year the day that you apologized to Mr. Anderson for giving them bad business advice?

A: I don't recall any such conversation.

57.3

Q: Are you certain you don't remember admitting giving Acme and Mr. Anderson bad advice and offering to remit back to Acme $5,000.00 of your fees for the previous year?

A: No, not at all.

Q: I have no further questions of this witness.

The defendant rested and the plaintiff opened their rebuttal case by calling Martin Anderson, President of Acme Paper Company. We pick up in the midst of the direct examination of Mr. Anderson.

Q: Do you know a person by the name of Georgia Meredith?

A: Yes, she was our accountant and business consultant up until the day of the fire.

Q: Was it the fire that ended her employment?

A: Oh, no. I fired her on the day of the fire.

Q: Why was that?

A: Well, Meredith came to my office on February 10th for our regular monthly meeting. During the meeting I told her that I was quite angry about the advice she had given us concerning some investments that she recommended and that we had followed through on. They turned out to be extremely bad investments and we took a real beating.

Q: How did she respond to your complaints?

A: She apologized. She admitted that it was bad advice, and that she had overlooked some very important significant data.

She also offered to give back her fee for
that advice, which was $5,000.00.

(Pause - 3)

Vignette 58

Defendant Joe Franklin was tried for armed robbery of a bank in June of last year, with two co-defendants. Despite claiming an alibi that they were out of the city on the day of the robbery, all three were found guilty. While the co-defendants' convictions were affirmed on appeal, Franklin's was reversed and remanded for a new trial. The government is now retrying Franklin. The government's first witness is Robert Sprague, the court clerk at the first trial.

Q: What is your name and occupation?

A: Robert Sprague; I am assistant Clerk of Court for the U.S. District Court.

Q: Directing your attention to June 10th of last year, where were you?

A: I was serving as a clerk in the courtroom of Judge Jones in the trial of the defendant and two co-defendants.

Q: Were you in court throughout the day?

A: I was present at the clerk's desk for every moment of the proceedings.

Q: Did the defendant Franklin's co-defendant, Jackson, testify at the trial?

A: Yes, he did. He testified in his own defense.

Q: Did Franklin's lawyer cross-examine Jackson?

A: No, the judge asked him if he wanted to cross-examine, but he said no.

Q: Who was Franklin's lawyer at the first trial?

A: Joe Darrow, who died last year.

Q: When co-defendant Jackson took the stand, what did he say?

(Pause - 1)

58.2

58.2

Vignette 59

Bob Rutherford is on trial for reckless homicide. The prosecution alleges that because Rutherford drove his car in a reckless manner, he crashed into another car, killing three passengers and severely injuring a fourth. The prosecution also alleges that Rutherford was guilty of a hit-and-run offense because he drove away immediately after the accident. The investigating police officer was Bill Friday. The prosecution has called Officer Friday.

We pick up in the midst of Officer Friday's testimony.

Q: Officer Friday, when you first approached the victims' car, was anyone alive?

A: Yes, everyone was alive, but they were all severely injured.

Q: Did anyone survive?

A: Yes. Though three people died within two hours of the accident, one survived.

Q: Did the driver die?

A: Yes, he did.

Q: Did you speak with the driver before he died?

A: Yes.

Q: What did he say?

A: Well, he asked me how badly he was hurt. I told him as nicely as I could that it looked bad and he might die.

Q: Did he say anything more?

A: He said that if he lived through this, he would kill Bob Rutherford, because Rutherford caused the accident.

(Pause - 1)

Q: Did you talk with anyone else?

A: Yes, I talked to the passenger in the front seat.

Q: Did he eventually die?

A: No, he's the one who survived.

Q: What was your conversation with him?

A: Well, I told him that he was badly injured and that he was probably wasn't going to make it. He nodded his head up and down.

Q: Was there anything else said?

A: Well, I asked him if he knew who drove the other car. He said that Bob Rutherford did it.

Q: How did he know it was Rutherford?

A: He said that he knew it was Rutherford because Rutherford is the only guy in town that drives as fast as the car that hit their car.

(Pause - 2)

Q: Did you talk with anyone else?

A: Yes, with Jane Simmons. She also died.

Q: What was that conversation?

A: I told her, "It looks bad. You're probably going to die." I then asked, "Was it Rutherford who hit you in his car?" She said, "yes," closed her eyes, and died.

(Pause - 3)

Vignette 60

At a trial of Richard Toney for bank robbery which occurred on January 15 of last year, the government has offered into evidence marked, stolen money linked to the bank robbery, which was found on Toney at the time of his arrest. Toney has testified that he won the stolen money from Jimmy King while shooting dice a few hours after the time of the robbery.

On rebuttal, the government offered evidence from other witnesses who said they had been part of the dice game in question and that the defendant Toney had <u>lost</u> money to King.

Toney now calls John Smith, an FBI agent on surrebuttal.

Q: What is your name and occupation?

A: John Smith. I am a Special Agent with the FBI.

Q: Do you know a Jimmy King?

A: Yes.

Q: How do you know him?

A: I arrested him for the bank robbery involved in this case, but I later had him released for insufficient evidence.

Q: When you had him in custody, did he make any statements to you?

A: Yes.

Q: What did he say?

A: After I gave him his Miranda warnings, he wanted to talk and he said that he had been gambling with the defendant Toney late on the night of January 15, and that he, King, had lost $1,000 to Toney. He also said Toney started the game with very little money.

(Pause - 1)

Vignette 61

This is a prosecution of a government official, Robert Billerman, for soliciting a bribe from a government contractor, Sam Carlin. Carlin testified for the government that the defendant requested a bribe, that he, Carlin, told his lawyer of the solicitation, contacted the FBI and then, under FBI surveillance and direction, paid the bribe. The defendant testified that it was Carlin who had initially offered the bribe to him and that he accepted the money, intending to report the bribe to his superiors. He was arrested by the FBI right after he got the money from Carlin but before he could make a report.

To rebut the defendant's testimony regarding who initiated the bribery conversation, the government called Carlin's lawyer, Schultz. The direct examination of Schultz follows:

Q: What is your name and occupation?

A: James Schultz, attorney at law.

Q: Do you know a Sam Carlin?

A: Yes, he is my most important client.

Q: Do you recall having a conversation with Mr. Carlin on January 28 of last year?

A: Yes, in my office.

Q: Who was present?

A: Just he and I were there.

Q: What did he say to you?

A: That the defendant solicited him for a bribe earlier that day.

(Pause - 1)

Vignette 62

John Carlson is on trial on charges of importation and sale of illicit drugs. Bob Smith, after being arrested with Carlson, was granted immunity in exchange for his testimony both before the grand jury and at trial. Smith's testimony before the grand jury provided the basis for Carlson's indictment. Smith is the government's first witness at trial.

Q: What is your name and occupation?

A: I am Bob Smith - unemployed at present.

Q: Mr. Smith, do you know the defendant John Carlson?

A: I ain't saying no more.

Q: Mr. Smith, I ask again, are you familiar with John Carlson?

A: I'm not going to testify.

Judge: Mr. Smith, you have been granted immunity. No harm can come to you from testifying and I order you to do so or be held in contempt.

A: Do anything you like, Judge, but Carlson threatened my kids if I talk and I'd rather go to jail than lose them.

Judge: Mr. Smith, you are in contempt of court.

A: I ain't talking.

Q: Your Honor, given this turn of events, the government would now offer a certified copy of the transcript of Mr. Smith's grand jury testimony in evidence.

(Pause - 1)

Review Vignette - I

The defendant, Jason Carson, is charged with larceny and extortion. The government claims that on or about January 29, YR-1 the defendant stole 100 pounds of uranium dioxide from the General Electric Company in Nita City and then extorted $100,000.00 from the company for its return. The first witness for the government is Robert Anderson.

Q: State your name and address for the record.

A: Robert Anderson, 32 Stony Brook Road, Nita City, Nita.

Q: You work for General Electric, don't you?

(Pause - 1)

A: Yes.

Q: What is your position?

A: I'm the plant manager.

Q: Were you so employed on January 29, YR-1?

A: Yes.

Q: What happened that day?

(Pause - 2)

A: I sat down at my desk and started to work on the annual report. I'd been working for about a half an hour when the intercom buzzed. My secretary said an envelope addressed to me had been found on the floor in the outer office. She said it was marked urgent.

(Pause - 3)

Q: What did you do?

A: Well, I thought I'd better have a look at it, so I told her to bring it in. A few seconds later she came into my office with a fat white envelope, legal size, which said "Anderson" and "urgent" on the outside.

(Pause - 4)

Q: What did you do?

A: I opened it. Inside was a ten- or twelve-page handwritten letter and a small vial containing uranium dioxide.

(Pause - 5)

Q: What happened next?

A: I read the letter.

Note: Assume you saw the letter during discovery. It is a threat to take the rest of the one hundred pounds of uranium the writer said he had actually stolen and mail it to the President and every senator and congressperson unless the company paid the writer $100,000. It is the only alleged communication between the defendant and the company.

Q: What did it say?

(Pause - 6)

Q: Mr. Anderson, I show you what has been marked as Government's Exhibit 1 for identification and ask you to take a good look at it. Do you recognize it?

A: Absolutely. This is the letter I was just talking about.

Q: Could you be mistaken?

A: No chance. The letter scared me so badly I spilled coffee all over it and I recognize the stain.

Q: Your Honor, the Government offers number 1 as a full exhibit.

(Pause - 7)

Q: After you read the letter, what did you do?

A: Aside from mopping up the coffee all over my desk, I had my secretary put a call through to Charles Rolland, our chief of security.

Q: Then what happened?

A: I told him what the letter said and he said, "Don't worry about this, boss. It looks like a crank letter, but I'll check into it."

(Pause - 8)

Q: Did you hear from him later?

A: He called to say it was no crank letter and that 100 pounds of uranium dioxide were missing.

(Pause - 9)

Q: That's all the questions I have. Thank you for coming to give your testimony, Mr. Anderson.

Court: Any questions?

Atty: Yes, your Honor.

Q: You saw the CBS Evening News the night of January 29, YR-1, didn't you?

A: Why, yes, I did.

Q: Dan Rather reported this story, didn't he?

A: Yes, he did.

Q: And didn't he say, and I quote, "It may well be that the man charged with this crime has done this country a big favor by exposing the lax security at plants which manufacture nuclear materials?"

(Pause - 10)

Q: By the way, Mr. Anderson, aren't you the same Robert Anderson who, on April 12, YR-11, was convicted of the felony of assaulting a Federal Officer in this very court and before this very judge, for which you received two years probation?

(Pause - 11)

A: You know, I was in a car accident three years ago and I can't remember anything that happened before that time, but I'm sure I wouldn't have done anything like that.

Q: Your Honor, we ask that you take judicial notice of the fact that this witness, Robert Anderson, entered a plea of guilty to assaulting a Federal Officer. We further ask you to instruct the jury that they must accept as true the fact that Mr. Anderson did, in fact, plead guilty to a felony.

(Pause - 12)

Def: We have no further questions of this witness.

Gov't: Just a few questions redirect, your Honor.

Court: You may proceed.

Q: Did you ever make arrangements to pay the money?

(Pause - 13)

A: Yes, with Agent Greenbaum of the FBI.

Q: No further questions of this witness.

Court: Very well. You may step down.

Court: We call Richard Greenbaum.

Q: Tell us about your occupation.

A: I am an FBI agent in Nita City, Nita. My actual title is Special Agent in Charge.

Q: Tell me about your training.

(Pause - 14)

A: Well, I got a J.D. from Nita Law School in YR-15 and took a job with the Nita Police Department as a police legal advisor. The work wasn't very challenging, so I applied to join the FBI in YR-14. They accepted me and I attended their six-month training course in Quantico, Virginia. The course covered all aspects of investigative work, including self-defense and weapons training. I worked at a number of offices until YR-3 when I received my current assignment.

Q: Calling your attention to 10:00 a.m. on January 29, YR-1. Tell the members of the jury what happened.

(Pause - 15)

A: I was in my office when I received a phone call from Charles Rolland out at the General Electric plant. He's the Manager of Security there. He told me I'd better get out there right away and that they had a problem he didn't want to discuss over the phone.

(Pause - 16)

Q: What did you do?

A: I got there as fast as I could and took with me two other special agents, Cagney and Lacey.

Q: What happened?

A: He showed me the note and I called Washington as I'm required to do whenever nuclear material has been stolen. I took the letter and also got a statement from Mr. Anderson and his secretary.

Q: Then what happened?

A: We had a tap put on the phone and waited for some contact from the extortionist, who had stated in the letter he would be back in touch to arrange an exchange of the uranium for the money. The company got the money from the local bank.

Q: Did you get a call?

A: At about 1:27 p.m. that day, the defendant called.

(Pause - 17)

Q: What did he say?

(Pause - 18)

A: He said he would exchange the money for a map to where the uranium was in the parking lot of the Nita Train Station at 2:30 p.m that day.

Q: What did you do?

A: We went to the train station parking lot and set up our strike force which consisted of all available FBI special agents, and State Troopers, and the Nita Police Department's SWAT team.

Q: And then?

A: Promptly at 2:30 p.m., Anderson was standing in the
    parking lot with the briefcase in his hands. In the
    case was $100,000 in small used bills. We had made
    a list of the serial numbers of each of the bills.

Q: Did anyone arrive?

A: Yes, at about 2:45 p.m. a short man, with a beard,
    wearing a tan trench coat, walked over to Mr.
    Anderson.

Q: About how far were you from where the defendant and
    Mr. Anderson were standing?

    (Pause - 19)

A: About 75 feet.

    (Pause - 20)

Q: What happened then?

A: Mr. Anderson handed the defendant the briefcase and
    the defendant gave Anderson a piece of paper. At
    that point, I had all units move in. The defendant
    didn't put up a fight.

Q: Looking around the courtroom, is the man who you saw
    talking to Mr. Anderson and later take the briefcase
    from him here today?

A: Yes, that's him over there.

Q: Let the record reflect the witness has identified
    the defendant.

Court: Hearing no objection, the record will so reflect.

Q: What did you do next?

A: We gave the defendant his rights. He said he wanted
    to talk to his lawyer so we asked him no questions.
    There were directions on the piece of paper. We
    followed them and recovered the missing uranium
    dioxide.

Q: What were the serial numbers of the bills in the
    briefcase Mr. Anderson carried?

A: I really can't remember all of them. They're in my
    report that I have here - would you like me to read
    them to you?

Q: Go ahead.

(Pause - 21)

Gov't: No further questions.

Def. Atty: We have a few questions on cross, your Honor.

Court: Proceed.

Q: Isn't it true that you previously described the man
    you saw in the field with Mr. Anderson as a tall man
    in a dark brown trench coat?

A: No.

Q: Doesn't your report filed with the FBI in the case
    say, and I quote, "The man was tall and wearing a
    dark brown trench coat?"

(Pause - 22)

A: Yes it does, but that's an error in the report.

Q: Isn't it true that when you arrested the defendant
    he looked confused?

A: I guess so, a little.

_____

Whereupon the trial recessed and during the recess the
defendant escaped.

_____

Review Vignette II

MICHAELS)
)
 V.   )
)
MICHAELS)

SUPERIOR COURT
NITA COUNTY

OCTOBER 30, YR-1

TRANSCRIPT OF THE PROCEEDINGS AT TRIAL

Clerk: Oyez, oyez, oyez. The civil term of the Superior Court is now open and in session. All persons having cause before this court draw nigh and give your attention according to law. The Honorable Voltaire Perkins presiding. Good morning, your Honor.

Court: Good morning. The first case on the trial docket, Mr. Clerk, appears to be the matter of Michaels v. Michaels.

Clerk: That's correct, your Honor. Susan Michaels, plaintiff suing her husband, John Michaels, on the grounds of mental cruelty. Mr. Michaels has cross-filed on the grounds of abandonment.

Court: Are both parties ready?

Both Counsel: Yes, your Honor.

Court: Very well, Mr. Clerk, swear everyone who is going to testify.

Clerk: Will all witnesses who are going to testify in this matter please rise and raise your right hand? Do you all swear that the testimony you are about to give in this matter is the truth, the whole truth and nothing but the truth, so help you God?

Witnesses: I do. (in unison)

(Pause - 1)

Court: All right, let's proceed with an opening statement for the plaintiff.

Plaintiff's
Atty: May it please the Court. Members of the jury.
       As counsel for the plaintiff, Susan Michaels,
       it is my responsibility to briefly outline her
       position in this matter. Through a number of
       witnesses including Susan Michaels, Dr. Horace
       Johnson and prominent members of this
       community, we will show that the defendant,
       Mr. John Michaels, inflicted great and
       unnecessary abuse upon his wife.

(Pause - 2)

The actions of the defendant, extending over a
significant period of time, drove Susan Michaels to
the brink of a complete emotional collapse and
rendered her incapable of tending to the needs of
her three young children. By publicly insulting her
as a wife and mother, by privately accusing her of
infidelity without cause and by neglecting his
marital duties, Mr. Michaels has made it clear that
he has no intention of meeting his responsibilities
as husband and father.

(Pause - 3)

Despite her persistent efforts to reconcile their
differences, Mr. Michaels and his representative
have failed to reach a negotiated accord.

(Pause - 4)

Forced into this proceeding, we are confident that
you will accept the facts as presented by Susan
Michaels and render judgment on her behalf. Thank
you.

Court: You may call your first witness, counsel.

Q: Very well, your Honor. The plaintiff calls Reginald
    Hall. Mr. Hall, will you please state your name for
    the record?

A: Reginald W. Hall.

Q: Where do you live, Mr. Hall?

A: 115 Willow Haven Rd.

Q: And you are Vice President of Continental
    Construction Co. and have been so employed for about
    ten years, is that right?

(Pause - 5)

A: That's correct.

Q: And you are acquainted with Susan Michaels and with
    her husband, John Michaels?

(Pause - 6)

A: Yes, I've known Susan most of her life. As for
    John, I've only known him for approximately eight
    years. But he's not very friendly, so I don't know
    him very well.

(Pause - 7)

Q: Mr. Hall, have you been to visit Ed at the Michaels'
    home in Longmeadow that was purchased for them by
    Susan's father?

(Pause - 8)

A: Oh yes, on a number of occasions.

Q: Have you visited there recently?

A: Yes, I have.

Q: What happened during one of your recent visits to
    the Michaels' home?

(Pause - 9)

A: I can remember being invited over to Susan's for a
    dinner party along with a number of friends from the
    Club. As usual, Susan had prepared a lovely meal
    and was being a charming and gracious hostess. She
    takes such good care of her home and family, you
    know. In any event, we had delayed dinner in hopes
    that John would arrive. Just as we had about given
    up, John stormed in from God knows where, looking
    like a wild man, shouting at Susan in vile language
    and then slammed the door and went out.

(Pause - 10)

Q: What did you and the other guests think about this
    incident?

(Pause - 11)

A: Well, naturally we were embarrassed for poor Susan and sympathized with her predicament.

Q: What did Mrs. Michaels do at that point?

A: Although mortified and quite upset, she struggled on. I remember her saying, "I don't know what I'm going to do. He's always doing things like that. It's so embarrassing."

(Pause - 12)

Q: So it's your testimony that Mr. Michaels deliberately embarrassed his wife in public and caused her great mental distress?

(Pause - 13)

A: Yes, it is.

Q: Do you have information that such occurrences were commonplace in the public and private lives of the Michaels?

A: Yes, Susan complained to me on several occasions.

(Pause - 14)

Q: Thank you, Mr. Hall. I have nothing further.

Cross Examination of Reginald Hall

Q: Mr. Hall, you've known Mrs. Michaels for quite some time?

A: All of her life, 28 or 29 years, I guess.

Q: And you are a close friend of hers and of her family, isn't that so?

(Pause - 15)

A: Yes, that's true.

Q: And it is also true that you are employed by Mrs. Michaels' father, J. Delbert Hathaway?

A: Yes, but........

Q: And this is the only position you have ever held since your graduation from college and it's your sole source of income, isn't it?

(Pause - 16)

A: Yes, but that has nothing to do with my testimony here.

(Pause - 17)

Q: However, it still remains that your employer is also the plaintiff's father?

A: Yes, I told you that.

Q: Now, turning to this "incident" that you claim occurred at the Michaels' home--you know, don't you, that Professor Michaels was involved in a tenure decision at the University?

(Pause - 18)

A: Well, I know now.

Q: At the time of this dinner party he was, wasn't he?

(Pause - 19)

A: I guess so.

Q: And when Professor Michaels came home that time he said, "Susan, I didn't know you had guests. You know I must work on my research and can't stay. Why didn't you tell me?" Didn't he make that statement?

(Pause - 20)

A: Well, he said something about working later.

Q: So, instead of cursing his wife as you stated on direct examination, all Professor Michaels did was to state that he had to work and couldn't stay for dinner, isn't that right?

(Pause - 21)

A: Well, his tone was clearly abusive and accusatory.

(Pause - 22)

Q: Isn't it true, Mr. Hall, that you've recently been divorced by your wife of 12 years?

Q2: Question irrelevant.

A: I'll connect this up in a few questions, your Honor.

(Pause - 23)

Q: And isn't it true that one of the grounds for the divorce was the claim by your wife that you spent too much time at the Club with Mrs. Michaels and others?

A: No, that's not true at all. She didn't like me going to the Club.

Q: In any event, in addition to your affection for Mrs. Michaels and her parents, it is also true that you've never liked Mr. Michaels, have you?

(Pause - 24)

A: I wouldn't say that.

Q: But you do believe that he doesn't fit in with your social group at the Club?

A: Well, he's not very athletic and he is a bit more academic than our crowd. But that doesn't mean I don't like him. As I said, he's not very friendly so I don't really know him.

(Pause - 25)

Q: I have nothing further of this witness.

Court: You may call your next witness.

Q: The plaintiff calls Dr. Horace Johnson. Would you please state your name and business address?

A: Horace B. Johnson and my office is in Suite 1500, Medical Arts Building, Hospital Drive.

Q: What is your profession?

A: I am a physician, specializing in the practice of psychiatry.

Q: Have you come to court today prepared to state an opinion as to Mrs. Michaels' mental condition?

A: Yes.

Q: Let's talk about your qualifications to come to such an opinion, Dr. Johnson. Are you licensed to practice medicine in the state?

A: Yes.

Q: When were you licensed?

A: In YR-15.

Q: Of what medical school are you a graduate?

A: Duke University Medical School.

Q: And where did you intern following medical school?

(Pause - 26)

A: At Temple University Hospital in Philadelphia.

Q: Following your internship, did you undertake a residency?

A: Yes, I did.

Q: Doctor, is a residency a course of study and practical experience for a period of years under the supervision of specialists in a specific field?

(Pause - 27)

A: Yes.

Q: And you specialized in psychiatry?

(Pause - 28)

A: That's correct.

Q: Where and for how long did you serve your residency?

(Pause - 29)

A: At Duke University Hospital for three years.

Q: Doctor, what is the American Board of Psychiatry?

A: This is a national organization of psychiatrists who have passed comprehensive written and oral examinations in the field of psychiatry.

Q: Are all doctors who specialize in psychiatry members of the American Board of Psychiatry?

A: No.

Q: Are you certified by the American Board of Psychiatry, Dr. Johnson?

A: Yes, I am.

Q: What additional educational experience do you have, doctor?

(Pause - 30)

A: Well, I spent a year at the University of Prague Medical School in advanced experimental work in psychoanalysis.

Q: Do you belong to any medical societies?

A: Yes, American Medical Association, the State Medical Association, and the County Medical Society.

Q: Are you on the staff of any hospital?

A: Yes, I am.

Q: Which hospital is that?

A: I am on the staff of the Nita University Hospital and associate director of the psychiatry department.

Q: Your Honor, I move that Dr. Johnson be declared an expert witness in the field of psychiatry.

Court: Any objection?

Q2: No, your Honor.

Court: Dr. Johnson may be qualified as an expert in
       the field of psychiatry. You may proceed.

Q: Thank you. Dr. Johnson, are you professionally
    acquainted with the plaintiff, Susan Michaels?

A: Yes, she is one of my patients.

Q: What was Mrs. Michaels' condition when she first
    came under your care in March of YR-3?

(Pause - 31)

A: She was extremely depressed.

Q: Can you be more specific?

A: Not without my file and notes concerning her case.

Q: Dr. Johnson, I have here your notes from your first
    visit with Mrs. Michaels on March 21, YR-2. Looking
    at them now, can you be more specific?

A: Yes, it says here that "patient very depressed and
    at moderate to advanced stage of melancholy due to
    an apparent failure of her marriage."

(Pause - 32)

Q: Did she give you a reason for this breakdown in her
    marriage?

A: Yes. She stated that her husband abused her,
    accusing her of infidelity and failure to care for
    their three children or their home. Also she said
    that he showed no interest in her, sexually or
    socially.

(Pause - 33)

Q: Did you take any steps to assist Mrs. Michaels?

A: Yes, I did. We set up regular visitations for
    psychiatric counseling, I prescribed medications--a
    mild tranquilizer--and I attempted to get her
    husband to participate in joint counseling.

Q: What attempts did you make to get the cooperation of
    her husband?

A: Well, with Mrs. Michaels' permission and encouragement, I called him to see if we could arrange a conference. When I finally reached him he said that it was none of my business what he was doing, that he didn't need psychiatric help and to confine myself to treating his wife.

(Pause - 34)

Q: Did you tell Mr. Michaels the serious nature of her mental problems and possible complications if he ignored her request?

(Pause - 35)

A: Yes, of course.

Q: So despite your warning, Mr. Michaels refused this attempt at reconciliation and counseling?

(Pause - 36)

A: That's right.

Q: Dr. Johnson, are you aware that at some point Mrs. Michaels left her husband?

(Pause - 37)

A: Yes, that was in the latter part of July, YR-2. She saw me before she left and I concurred in her judgement.

(Pause - 38)

Q: Why did you agree with the separation?

A: Because, despite my efforts, her mental condition had deteriorated and, in my opinion, the only chance she had to avoid a complete collapse was to dissolve the relationship with her husband.

Q: Doctor, is it your opinion that Mrs. Michaels' mental condition is related to her husband's attitudes and actions toward her?

(Pause - 39)

A: Yes, indeed. Her mental health was, and clearly is, affected by her husband's treatment of her.

Q: Doctor, do you have an opinion regarding whether or not the continuation of the marriage is conducive to the plaintiff's mental health?

(Pause - 40)

A: Yes, I do.

Q: What is that opinion?

A: I believe that to continue the marriage will result in permanent mental harm to Mrs. Michaels.

Q: Thank you, Dr. Johnson. I have nothing further.

Cross-Examination of Dr. Horace Johnson

Defendant's Atty: Dr. Johnson, you stated on direct examination that Mrs. Michaels' mental condition is related to treatment by her husband?

A: That is correct.

Q: Doctor, have you always been of that opinion?

A: Yes, I have.

Q: Directing your attention to the evening of Sunday, July 29, YR-2, you were called to the Psychiatric Rehabilitation Center at University Hospital, weren't you?

A: Yes.

Q: At that time you treated the plaintiff, Susan Michaels, correct?

A: I saw her there. She couldn't reach me so she went to the hospital and they called me.

(Pause - 41)

Q: Is it fair to say that she was in an extremely disturbed state at the time?

A: Well, I'm not sure I'd use those words. She was upset.

Q: Perhaps this will help you recall it better. I have here a standard University Hospital Psychiatric Evaluation form, signed by you and dated July 29, YR-2, relating to Susan Hathaway Michaels. In this report you wrote, "Susan very depressed. Claims that once again the children are too much for her and that if she can't get away from them, I'll go crazy. Have advised staying away from home until we can stabilize her condition. Have reached her parents to see if they can help since Susan unwilling to accept inpatient hospital care. Medication prescribed." Now, Doctor, in this report, you give an entirely different reason for Mrs. Michaels' departure from her home, don't you?

(Pause - 42)

A: Well, it may appear that way, but that report doesn't...

(Pause - 43)

Q: There's no need for explanations, Doctor. You know J. Delbert Hathaway, the plaintiff's father, don't you?

A: Just slightly. He is a member of the University Board of Trustees and is a city councilman. I've met him at various functions.

Q: Doctor, are you aware of the Continental Endowment Fund?

A: Yes. It awarded me and two of my colleagues a small grant last year to continue our research into the use of hypnosis as a psychological technique equally effective as many medications.

Q: The plaintiff's father is the principal contributor to the Fund and sits on its board of directors, doesn't he?

A: Yes, I know that.

Q: And isn't it true, Dr. Johnson, that your grant is up for renewal within the next six months?

Q2: Objection, irrelevant.

(Pause - 44)

64.12

A: Yes, but I'm not sure I know what you're driving at.

Q: Isn't it reasonable to believe that your testimony here today is an attempt to protect Mr. Hathaway's daughter and thereby favorably influence his decision on your grant application?

(Pause - 45)

A: Certainly not! I resent your insinuation.

Q: Resent it or not, Doctor, it's a reasonable interpretation of the facts.

(Pause - 46)

Now, have you continued to treat Mrs. Michaels since July 29, YR-2?

A: Yes, I have.

Q: In the course of treatment, has she mentioned to you anything about having an affair with another man?

(Pause - 47)

A: Well, she told me that since her husband has failed for many months to touch or sleep with her that she has been sexually deprived and I agree with her.

(Pause - 48)

Q: But she has told you that she has initiated a sexual relationship with another man, hasn't she?

(Pause - 49)

A: Not in so many words, but in substance that's true.

Q: So in reality, Doctor, the cause of this marital breakup is Mrs. Michaels' failure to care for her children and her illicit activity, not her husband's attitude toward her?

(Pause - 50)

A: No, I wouldn't agree with that statement.

Q: I have no further questions at this time.